THE OFFICIAL
JOHN WAYNE
5-INGREDIENT
HOMESTYLE
COOKBOOK

Simple Recipes and Heartfelt Stories from Duke's Family Kitchen

John Wayne checks in on his cattle at the 26 Bar Ranch.

KEEPING THINGS SIMPLE

My father knew the family that gathered around the table together shared much more than good food—they made memories, gave each other honest advice and strengthened the bonds of love through thick and thin. That's why we've collected these delicious, authentic recipes that you can whip up with just five or fewer ingredients, allowing you to focus on what really matters most—spending quality time with family and friends. From savory sides to mouth-watering main meals and even decadent desserts, this book will be your go-to when it comes to no-fuss dishes that come together in a pinch so you can enjoy more time with your loved ones, just like Duke would want.

Dig in.

Ethan

—ETHAN WAYNE

John Wayne gathers around the table with Marisa, Pilar and Ethan.

❖ TABLE OF CONTENTS ❖

10
Breakfast

162
Snacks

192
Desserts

32
Soups & Salads

62
Starters

94
Mains

222
Salsas, Sauces & More

Chisum's Chilaquiles, page 22

The Best Darn Chocolate Chip Cookies, page 202

For your convenience, we've included icons to highlight the main ingredients of every recipe. To keep things simple, these icons won't feature common kitchen essentials such as cooking oils and vinegars, salt and pepper, water, pots, pans or toothpicks.

John Wayne takes in the surf aboard the *Wild Goose*. Captain Bert Minshall recounts sailing the high seas with the the unforgettable film legend in his 1992 memoir, *On Board with the Duke: John Wayne and the Wild Goose*.

Brannigan's
Breakfast
Sandwiches, pg. 28

BREAKFAST

TASTY MEALS THAT WILL START YOUR DAY OFF ON THE RIGHT BOOT.

Rio Bravo
BISCUITS & GRAVY

WHETHER YOU'RE FEEDING A SHERIFF, A BARTENDER OR A YOUNG GUNSLINGER, EVERYONE CAN AGREE ON THE DELICIOUSNESS OF THIS CLASSIC DISH.

Serves 6

PROVISIONS

Biscuits

- 1¼ cups cold milk
- 1½ Tbsp. white vinegar
- 3 cups all-purpose flour
- 4 tsp. baking powder
- ¾ tsp. kosher or fine sea salt
- ¾ cup (1½ sticks) cold butter, cut into pieces
- ¼ cup (½-stick) melted butter

Gravy

- 1 lb. breakfast sausage
- ⅓ cup all-purpose flour
- 4 cups milk
- 1½ tsp. black pepper
- ¾ tsp. kosher or fine sea salt

DIRECTIONS

BISCUITS

1. Preheat oven to 400 degrees F and line two baking sheets with parchment paper.

2. Combine the milk and vinegar and let sit 5 minutes to "sour."

3. Combine the flour, baking powder and salt in a large mixing bowl. Add the butter and cut into the flour mixture with a pastry cutter. Drizzle in the soured milk and stir until the dough comes together.

4. Drop large spoonfuls of the dough onto the prepared baking sheets. Bake for 15 to 17 minutes or until golden brown. As soon as the biscuits come out of the oven, brush with melted butter.

GRAVY

1. Break up the sausage into a large skillet and cook over medium heat until browned and no longer pink. Reduce heat to medium-low and sprinkle the flour over the sausage. Cook for 1 minute, stirring.

2. Add the milk while stirring and cook until thickened, about 10 minutes. Stir in the pepper and salt and serve the gravy over the hot biscuits.

Big Jake's
BREAKFAST CASSEROLE

WHEN YOU WAKE UP WITH A BIG APPETITE, YOU CAN COUNT ON THIS DISH TO GET THE JOB DONE.

Serves 8-10

PROVISIONS

2 Tbsp. vegetable oil

1 (30-oz.) bag frozen hash browns

1½ tsp. kosher or fine sea salt, divided

1 tsp. black pepper, divided

2 lbs. breakfast sausage

2 cups (8 oz.) grated Mexican cheese blend

6 large eggs

2 cups milk

DIRECTIONS

1. Preheat oven to 350 degrees F and oil a 9- by 12-inch (or similar) baking dish.

2. Heat the oil in a large skillet with a lid over medium. Add the hash browns, ½ tsp. salt and ½ tsp. pepper and toss to coat. Cook, covered, for 10 to 15 minutes, flipping the hash browns occasionally as they brown on the bottom.

3. Crumble the sausage into a large skillet over medium-high heat. Cook, breaking it up until no longer pink, about 10 minutes. Drain well, then add to the hash browns along with the cheese and stir well. Spread the mixture evenly into the prepared dish.

4. Beat the eggs and milk together with 1 tsp. salt and ½ tsp. pepper. Pour over the sausage mixture and bake for 35 to 40 minutes.

John Wayne and the cast of *Big Jake* (1971).

DID YOU KNOW?

Duke's fourth and final number one box office hit, *Big Jake* (1971), was the last film in which Duke appeared onscreen with Maureen O'Hara and Christopher Mitchum.

McLintock's
MUSHROOM BACON FRITTATA

AS THIS RECIPE PROVES, NOTHING BRINGS A FAMILY TOGETHER LIKE A SIZZLING SAVORY MEAL IN THE MORNING.

Serves 4-6

PROVISIONS

1 tsp. olive oil

4 slices thick-cut bacon, diced

16 oz. sliced mushrooms

1 tsp. kosher or fine sea salt

½ tsp. pepper

10 large pastured eggs

1 cup Parmesan cheese, grated

DIRECTIONS

1. Heat 1 tsp. olive oil in a 10-inch oven-proof skillet over medium. Add the bacon and cook for 2 minutes. Add the mushrooms, salt and pepper. Cook, stirring occasionally, until the mushrooms have released their liquid and the liquid has evaporated, 12 to 14 minutes. Remove pan from the heat.

2. Preheat oven to 400 degrees F.

3. Lightly beat the eggs and pour over the mushrooms and bacon. Sprinkle Parmesan cheese over the top of the eggs and bake for 10 minutes or until the eggs are set. Serve immediately.

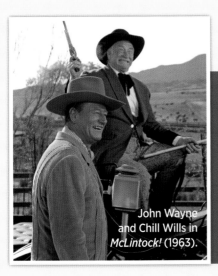

John Wayne and Chill Wills in *McLintock!* (1963).

DID YOU KNOW?

Three of Duke's children participated in the making of *McLintock!*: Michael Wayne served as producer, while Patrick and Aissa Wayne shared the screen with their father as Devlin Warren and Alice Warren, respectively.

17

El Dorado
TOSTADA

START THE DAY OFF RIGHT WITH SOME SOUTH-OF-THE-BORDER FLAVOR.

Serves 4

PROVISIONS

Vegetable or extra-virgin olive oil

4 corn tortillas

12 Tbsp. refried beans

8 Tbsp. Mexican blend grated cheese

8 Tbsp. prepared salsa

4 large eggs

Kosher or fine sea salt

Black pepper

DIRECTIONS

1. Position oven rack about 6 inches from the broiler. Preheat the broiler. Line a baking sheet with parchment paper.

2. Heat about 1 Tbsp. of oil in a small skillet until very hot. Add the tortillas, one at a time, and fry until golden brown and crispy on one side, about 1 minute. Flip and fry the other side for 30 seconds. Pat off the excess oil with a paper towel and place on the baking sheet. Repeat with remaining tortillas, adding more oil if needed.

3. Spread the beans evenly over the top of the tortillas and sprinkle with the cheese. Broil for about 2 minutes or until the cheese starts to melt. Top with the salsa.

4. Heat a little oil in a large skillet over medium. Fry the eggs and place on top of the tostada. Season with salt and pepper to taste.

John Wayne and Robert Mitchum in *El Dorado* (1967).

DID YOU KNOW?

Before starring as Cole Thornton, Duke read the script for *El Dorado* and expressed interest in playing the part of Sheriff J.P. Harrah. The role eventually went to Robert Mitchum.

Helen Parrish, David Rollins, John Wayne and Marguerite Churchill head west in *The Big Trail* (1930). It would be another nine years before Duke shot to stardom as the Ringo Kid in John Ford's *Stagecoach* (1939).

Chisum's CHILAQUILES

THE SMELL OF THIS DISH COOKING IN THE SKILLET IS SURE TO GET EVERYONE OUT OF BED IN A HURRY.

Serves 6

PROVISIONS

12 corn tortillas

Corn oil

1½-2 cups Red Hot Chili Sauce (pg. 242) or Salsa Verde (pg. 246)

½ tsp. kosher or fine sea salt

6 large eggs

½ tsp. black pepper

½ cup chopped cilantro leaves

½ cup crumbled cotija cheese

DIRECTIONS

1. Cut the tortillas into 6 wedges. Pour enough oil into a large skillet to cover by ¼ of an inch. Heat over medium-high heat. When the oil is hot, drop the cut tortillas into the pan, working in batches so as not to over-crowd the pan. Fry until golden brown on one side, 1 to 2 minutes, then flip and fry on the other side until golden brown, another 1 to 2 minutes.

2. Remove to a paper towel-lined plate to drain and sprinkle with a little salt. Repeat with remaining tortillas until they are all fried. Drain off all but 1 Tbsp. of oil.

3. Add the red chili sauce or salsa verde and cook for 2 minutes. Reduce the heat to medium-low. Whisk the eggs with ½ tsp. salt and ½ tsp. pepper. Pour into the hot sauce and cook, stirring occasionally, until the eggs are fully incorporated into the sauce and set, about 10 minutes. Add the tortillas back into the pan and stir to make sure they are fully coated with sauce.

4. Top with the cilantro and cheese and serve immediately.

John Wayne in *Chisum* (1970).

DID YOU KNOW?

Along with *The Sons of Katie Elder* (1965) and *Cahill: U.S. Marshal* (1973), *Chisum* (1970) was one of several Duke flicks filmed in the town of Chupaderos in Durango, Mexico.

Cowboy QUICHE

SADDLE UP FOR A SAVORY MEAL YOU WON'T SOON FORGET, PILGRIM!

Serves 6

PROVISIONS

8 slices thick-cut bacon, cut into ½-inch pieces

2 large yellow onions, thinly sliced

1 tsp. kosher or fine sea salt, divided

1 tsp. pepper, divided

2 cups (8-oz.) grated sharp cheddar cheese

8 large eggs

1½ cups heavy cream

DIRECTIONS

1. Preheat oven to 350 degrees F and grease a 9- to 10-inch deep-dish pie plate.

2. Place the bacon in a large cold skillet. Turn heat to medium-high and cook the bacon just until it starts to render its fat, about 2 minutes. Add the onions on top of the bacon, sprinkle with ½ tsp. salt and ½ tsp. pepper, and toss to coat. Lower the heat to medium and cook, uncovered, stirring occasionally for 20 minutes or until the onions are soft and slightly golden and the bacon is starting to brown.

3. Using a slotted spoon or tongs, transfer the mixture to the prepared pie plates, getting as little of the bacon grease as possible. Top with the cheese.

4. Beat the eggs and cream with ½ tsp. salt and ½ tsp. pepper. Pour over the cheese.

5. Bake for 35 to 40 minutes or until the eggs are set and browned.

John Wayne in *The Man from Utah* (1934).

Quirt Evans's
MAPLE BACON PANCAKES

THESE SWEET AND SAVORY TREATS WILL HAVE YOUR FAMILY FLIPPING OUT OVER FLAPJACKS IN A WHOLE NEW WAY.

Serves 4-6

PROVISIONS

12 slices thick-cut bacon

2 cups pancake mix

1½ cups milk

¼ cup maple syrup, plus more for serving

2 large eggs

DIRECTIONS

1. Dice the bacon and place in a cold skillet. Cook over medium heat, stirring occasionally, until browned and crispy, about 10 minutes. Using a slotted spoon, remove the bacon and place on a paper towel lined plate to drain. Reserve the bacon grease.

2. Heat a non-stick skillet over medium until a drop of water sprinkled on the skillet sizzles immediately.

3. Meanwhile, combine the pancake mix, milk, maple syrup and eggs in a mixing bowl, stirring well. Save about ¼ of the bacon bits to garnish the pancakes and stir the rest into the batter.

4. Coat the hot skillet with about 1 Tbsp. bacon grease. Let it heat up, then ladle in ¼ cup of batter per pancake. Cook 2 to 3 minutes or until the edges look dry and the bottom is golden brown. Flip and cook until the bottoms are golden brown, about 2 to 3 minutes. Keep the pancakes warm while cooking the rest of the batter.

5. Serve the pancakes with the reserved bacon bits and maple syrup.

John Wayne and Gail Russell in *Angel and the Badman* (1947).

Brannigan's BREAKFAST SANDWICHES

THESE HEARTY SANDWICHES ARE SO GOOD, THEY OUGHT TO BE OUTLAWED.

Serves 6

PROVISIONS

6 English muffins

½ cup butter (1 stick), melted

6 slices American cheese

6 slices Canadian bacon

6 large eggs

Kosher or fine sea salt, to taste

Black pepper, to taste

DIRECTIONS

1. Heat a griddle over medium until a drop of water sprinkled on the skillet sizzles immediately.

2. Separate the English muffin halves and butter the cut sides. Place cut side down on the griddle and toast for 1 to 2 minutes or until golden brown. Remove and immediately place a slice of American cheese on the bottom half of the muffin.

3. Brush the griddle with butter and cook the Canadian bacon until warm and lightly browned on each side, 1 to 2 minutes. Place the Canadian bacon slices on top of the cheese.

4. Brush the griddle with more butter. Butter 6 large Mason jar rings or egg rings and place on the griddle. Crack an egg into each ring and sprinkle with a pinch of salt and pepper. Cook until 80 percent of the whites are set, about 3 minutes. Remove the rings and flip the eggs and cook for 1 minute. Place the eggs on top of the Canadian bacon. Put the top of the English muffin on the egg, then brush with butter and place on the griddle for 1 to 2 minutes to brown the top.

5. Serve sandwiches immediately or wrap in foil to keep warm.

John Wayne and Judy Geeson in *Brannigan* (1975).

Rancher's SCRAMBLE

THIS HEARTY DISH IS EXACTLY WHAT YOU NEED BEFORE A HARD-DAY'S WORK.

Serves 4

PROVISIONS

2 medium Yukon Gold potatoes, scrubbed

1 small yellow onion, diced

1 red bell pepper, diced

1½ tsp. kosher or fine sea salt, divided

1 Tbsp. olive oil

2 oz. cooked ham or Canadian bacon

½ tsp. pepper

6 large eggs

DIRECTIONS

1. Cut the potatoes into 1-inch pieces and place in a medium skillet with the onion and bell pepper. Add 1 tsp. salt and pour in enough water to just cover the vegetables.

2. Bring to a boil over high heat, then reduce to a simmer and cover the pan and let cook for 10 minutes or until the potatoes are tender. Drain off the water, add the olive oil and ham and stir. Cook over high heat, stirring once or twice, for 2 minutes.

3. Whisk the eggs with ½ tsp. salt and ½ tsp. pepper. Reduce the heat to low, then add the eggs and let cook, stirring occasionally, until the eggs are set for about 5 minutes. Serve immediately.

Duke shares a moment with some of the workers at his 26 Bar Ranch.

DID YOU KNOW?

When he wasn't filming, Duke enjoyed spending time in the great outdoors at his Arizona cattle ranch, the 26 Bar Ranch, where he raised prized Hereford cattle with partner and ranch manager Louis Johnson.

Spicy Tomato Soup,
pg. 56

SOUPS & SALADS

**LOAD UP ON BOWLS FULL OF FLAVOR
THAT WON'T WEIGH YOU DOWN.**

Seabees
BLACK BEAN SOUP

A BIG BOWL OF THIS CLASSIC IS SURE TO SATISFY.

Serves 4

PROVISIONS

2 (15-oz.) cans black beans,
drained and rinsed

2 cups chicken or vegetable stock

½ cup prepared salsa

1 tsp. ground cumin

Kosher or fine sea salt,
to taste

Black pepper, to taste

½ recipe Cantina Lime Sour
Cream (see pg. 236)

DIRECTIONS

1. Pour 1 can of black beans in a blender with the stock, salsa and ground cumin. Blend until smooth.

2. Pour into a saucepan with the other can of beans and heat over medium. Taste and add salt and pepper if needed. Top with dollops of Cantina Lime Sour Cream.

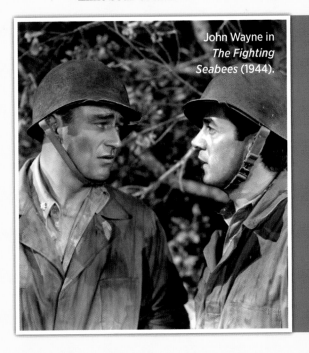

John Wayne in
*The Fighting
Seabees* (1944).

DID YOU KNOW?

Filmed while American troops were still fighting in the Pacific, the gung-ho WWII film *The Fighting Seabees* is one of few films in which John Wayne's character meets his end onscreen. In this case, he's taken down by a Japanese sniper while riding atop a bulldozer.

Cheesy
POTATO SOUP

AFTER TRYING THIS HEARTY FAVORITE, YOUR FAMILY WILL BE LINING UP FOR SECONDS IN NO TIME.

— *Serves 6* —

PROVISIONS

2 lbs. russet potatoes, peeled and diced into 1-inch pieces

4 cups chicken or vegetable broth

6 green onions, thinly sliced, white and green parts separated

2 Tbsp. Cajun seasoning

1 cup plus 6 Tbsp. shredded cheddar cheese

Kosher or fine sea salt, to taste

Black pepper, to taste

DIRECTIONS

1. Combine the potatoes, broth, white parts of the onions and Cajun seasoning in a large stock pot and bring to a boil over medium-high heat. Reduce heat, cover and simmer, stirring occasionally until potatoes are very tender, about 15 minutes.

2. Transfer mixture to a blender and puree until smooth. Return to the pot, stir in 1 cup cheese and heat over low until the cheese is melted. Taste and add salt and pepper if needed.

3. Serve the soup garnished with 1 Tbsp. cheese and the green parts of the onions.

Max Terhune, John Wayne and Ray Corrigan in *Overland Stage Raiders* (1938).

Paul Fix, John Wayne, Gabby Hayes and Raymond Hatton in *Tall in the Saddle* (1944). The film marked the final collaboration between Duke and Hayes, who first met while working on the set of *Riders of Destiny* (1933).

CORN & BLACK BEAN SALAD

SADDLE UP—THIS SALAD WILL TAKE YOUR TASTEBUDS ON A RIDE.

Serves 4-6

PROVISIONS

1 (15-oz.) can black beans, rinsed and drained

2 cups fresh or frozen and thawed corn kernels

1 (10-oz.) can tomato and chilies, drained

½ small red onion, finely diced

1 tsp. ground cumin

2 Tbsp. olive oil

1 Tbsp. red wine vinegar

Kosher or fine sea salt, to taste

Black pepper, to taste

DIRECTIONS

1. Combine beans, corn, tomato and chilies, onion, cumin, oil and vinegar in a medium mixing bowl. Season to taste with salt and pepper.

John Wayne, Montgomery Clift and Walter Brennan in *Red River* (1948).

DID YOU KNOW? 11 years after making his Broadway debut in the 1935 musical *Jubilee*, Montgomery Clift hit a new career milestone when he filmed his first movie—alongside John Wayne, no less—*Red River*, released in 1948.

Cahill's
CORN CHOWDER

THIS DELICIOUS DISH WILL KEEP YOU WARM NO MATTER WHAT THE WEATHER IS OUTSIDE.

Serves 4-6

PROVISIONS

2 slices thick-cut bacon, diced

2 large Yukon gold potatoes, peeled and diced into 1-inch pieces

4 green onions, chopped, white and green parts separated

2 (14-oz.) cans creamed corn

1 cup water

1 cup half-and-half

1 tsp. kosher or fine sea salt

½ tsp. black pepper

DIRECTIONS

1. Place the bacon in a cold large stockpot and cook on medium heat until the bacon is crisp. With a slotted spoon, remove the bacon to a paper towel-lined plate to drain. Leave 2 Tbsp. of the bacon fat in the pot.

2. Add the potatoes and the white parts of the onions to the pot. Cook for 5 minutes. Add the creamed corn, water, half-and-half, salt and pepper. Increase heat to medium-high and bring to a boil. Reduce heat and simmer, stirring frequently, for 20 minutes or until potatoes are tender.

3. Top with the reserved bacon and green onions and serve.

John Wayne in *Cahill: U.S. Marshal* (1973).

Wayne Family Tip

Cans of creamed corn will definitely get the job done just fine, but if you have extra time on your hands, spring for using fresh corn. Steep the leftover corn cobs for a stock that'll lend your soup more flavor for little fuss.

PINEAPPLE BACON COLESLAW

ENJOY A TROPICAL TWIST ON THIS CLASSIC DISH.

Serves 6

PROVISIONS

4 slices thick-cut bacon, diced

1 (20-oz.) can pineapple chunks in juice

6 Tbsp. mayonnaise

1 (16-oz.) bag tricolor coleslaw mix

4 green onions, thinly sliced

1 tsp. kosher or fine sea salt

½ tsp. black pepper

DIRECTIONS

1. Place the bacon in a cold skillet over medium heat. Cook, stirring frequently, until the bacon is crisp, about 8 minutes. Drain on paper towels.

2. Drain the pineapple chunks and reserve 3 Tbsp. of juice. Whisk the juice with the mayonnaise.

3. In a large mixing bowl, combine the slaw mix with the bacon, pineapple, green onions, salt and pepper. Add the mayonnaise mixture and stir well to combine.

John Wayne and Duke Kahanamoku in *Wake of the Red Witch* (1948).

DID YOU KNOW?

In *Wake of the Red Witch*, Duke shares the screen with the legendary surfer and Olympic champion swimmer Duke Kahanamoku, whose wave riding exhibitions helped bring the Hawaiian sport to the world stage.

Country-style PASTA SALAD

SERVE THIS SURE-TO-SATISFY STARTER THE NEXT TIME YOU'RE HOSTING GUESTS AT THE HOMESTEAD.

Serves 6

PROVISIONS

Kosher or fine sea salt, to taste

12 oz. dried penne

4 slices thick-cut bacon, diced

1 cup grated cheddar cheese

½ pint cherry tomatoes,
cut into quarters

4-5 Tbsp. Buttermilk Chive Ranch
Dressing (see pg. 228)

Black pepper

DIRECTIONS

1. Bring a large pot of heavily
salted water to a boil. Cook the
penne according to the package
directions. Drain, rinse with
cold water and drain again. Put
pasta into a large mixing bowl.

2. Place the bacon in a large cold
skillet. Turn the heat to medium
and cook, stirring occasionally,
until crisp, about 8 minutes.
Drain on paper towels.

3. Add the bacon to the pasta along with the cheese and tomatoes. Stir,
then add the dressing and continue to stir. Season to taste with salt
and pepper.

4. Cover and refrigerate until serving.

John Wayne in *The Horse Soldiers* (1959)

ICEBERG WEDGE (DONOVAN) SALAD

WITH CRISPY BACON AND CREAMY RANCH DRESSING, THIS SALAD PACKS A FISTFUL OF FLAVOR.

Serves 4-6

PROVISIONS

4 slices thick-cut bacon, diced

1 head iceberg lettuce

1 pint cherry tomatoes, halved or quartered

½ cup Buttermilk Chive Ranch Dressing (see pg. 228)

DIRECTIONS

1. Place the bacon in a cold skillet. Turn the heat to medium and cook, stirring occasionally, until crisp, about 8 minutes. Drain on paper towels.

2. Cut the lettuce into 6 wedges. Place on a platter. Scatter the tomatoes and bacon over the lettuce and drizzle with the dressing.

John Wayne and the cast of *Donovan's Reef* (1963).

DID YOU KNOW?

Donovan's Reef was filmed on location on the island of Kauai, Hawaii. The Aloha state held a special place in Duke's heart and served as the site of his wedding to Pilar on November 1, 1954.

John Wayne and his wife
Pilar gather around the table
with their children Ethan,
Marisa and Aissa. Duke
named his son Ethan as a
tribute to his favorite role of
all time: Ethan Edwards in
The Searchers (1956).

Red, White & Blue
POTATO SALAD

AFTER THEY TASTE THIS ALL-AMERICAN DISH, YOUR FAMILY WILL STAND UP AND SALUTE YOU.

Serves 6

PROVISIONS

1½ lbs. tricolored small potatoes

Kosher or fine sea salt

3 Tbsp. red wine vinegar

3 Tbsp. olive oil

Freshly ground black pepper

½ medium red onion, diced

6 Tbsp. mayonnaise

1 Tbsp. yellow mustard

6 hard-boiled eggs, peeled and chopped

DIRECTIONS

1. Place the potatoes in a large pot and cover with 1 inch of cold water. Add 2 tsp. salt and bring to a boil. Let simmer until potatoes are fork tender, about 20 minutes. Drain and let cool until safe to handle but still warm.

2. In a large mixing bowl, whisk together the vinegar, olive oil, 2 tsp. salt and 1 tsp. pepper. Add the onion and stir to combine.

3. Cut the potatoes in half and add to the mixing bowl. Stir to combine, then let sit for a few minutes.

4. In a small bowl, combine the mayonnaise and mustard. Add the eggs to the potatoes, then the mayonnaise/mustard sauce, and gently stir to combine. Cover and refrigerate for at least 1 hour. Taste and adjust seasoning with more salt and pepper, if desired. Can be made a day ahead.

DID YOU KNOW?

In the *Sands of Iwo Jima,* Duke appears onscreen with Pfc. René Gagnon, a Marine who retrieved the first flag raised at Mount Suribachi during the Battle of Iwo Jima. The iconic photo captures the second flag-raising.

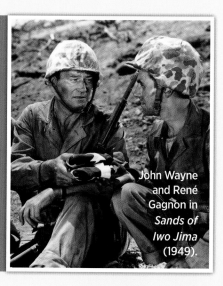

John Wayne and René Gagnon in *Sands of Iwo Jima* (1949).

Rooster's
ROASTED ONION SOUP

FILL YOUR HANDS (AND STOMACH) WITH A BIG BOWL OF THIS SAVORY SOUP.

Serves 4

PROVISIONS

2 large sweet onions, sliced

2 Tbsp. olive oil

2 cloves garlic, minced

½ tsp. kosher or fine sea salt

¼ tsp. black pepper

2 Tbsp. balsamic vinegar

4 cups beef broth

8 baguette slices, toasted

1 cup grated Gruyere cheese

DIRECTIONS

1. Preheat oven to 375 degrees F. Place onions in a 9- by 12-inch baking dish, add the olive oil, garlic, salt and pepper, then toss to coat. Roast for 45 to 50 minutes or until very soft and lightly browned, stirring occasionally.

2. Add the vinegar to the onions and stir, scraping up any browned bits. Transfer to a large stockpot with the beef broth and bring to a boil over medium-high heat. Reduce the heat and let simmer, covered, for 15 to 20 minutes. Adjust seasoning with more salt and pepper if desired.

3. Preheat the broiler and place the top rack about 6 inches from the heat source. Place the baguette slices on a foil-lined baking sheet. Divide the cheese evenly among the slices and broil for 2 to 3 minutes or until the cheese is melted and beginning to brown.

4. Pour the soup into bowls and top with 2 baguette slices per bowl.

John Wayne and Katharine Hepburn in *Rooster Cogburn* (1975).

Spicy
TOMATO SOUP

YOU AND YOURS WILL GET A REAL "KICK" OUT OF THIS TASTY TAKE ON AN OLD STANDARD.

Serves 4

PROVISIONS

2 Tbsp. olive oil

1 small yellow onion, diced

½ tsp. red pepper flakes

1 (28-oz.) can diced tomatoes

1 cup water

¼ cup fresh basil leaves

½ cup Cantina Lime Sour Cream (see pg. 236) or sour cream, plus more for serving

Kosher or fine sea salt, to taste

DIRECTIONS

1. In a large stockpot over medium heat, heat the olive oil until hot. Add the onion and red pepper flakes and cook, stirring occasionally, until the onions are very tender, about 10 minutes.

2. Add the tomatoes along with their juices and water and bring to a boil. Reduce heat to low and simmer for 30 minutes.

3. Pour into a blender with the basil and puree until smooth. Add the sour cream and blend. Taste and add salt as needed. Return the soup to the pot and warm over low heat.

3. Serve with a dollop of sour cream.

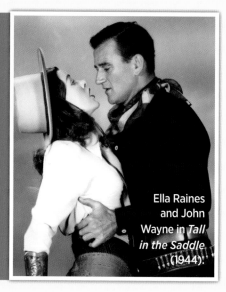

DID YOU KNOW?

In 1944, Duke's *Tall in the Saddle* costar Ella Raines graced the cover of *Life* magazine, starred in four other films including the Franchot Tone film noir *Phantom Lady* and appeared as a pin-up girl in the G.I. magazine *Yank*.

Ella Raines and John Wayne in *Tall in the Saddle* (1944).

SPINACH SALAD
with Warm Bacon Dressing

**PERHAPS THE MOST SAVORY SALAD EVER CONCEIVED,
THIS CROWD-PLEASER FEATURES TASTY PAN DRIPPINGS AND HOMEMADE BACON BITS.**

Serves 4

PROVISIONS

8 slices thick-cut bacon, diced

3 Tbsp. red wine vinegar

1 tsp. sugar

8 oz. baby spinach,
washed and dried well

4 hard-boiled eggs, sliced

4 green onions, thinly sliced

Kosher or fine sea salt, to taste

Black pepper, to taste

DIRECTIONS

1. Place the bacon in a cold skillet and turn the heat on to medium. Cook, stirring frequently, until crisp, about 8 to 10 minutes. Remove the bacon with a slotted spoon and drain on paper towels.

2. Leave 3 Tbsp. of the bacon grease in the pan, add the vinegar and sugar, and cook over medium heat for a minute.

3. Place the spinach in a serving bowl, add the dressing from the pan and toss. Add the bacon, eggs and green onions and toss gently. Season to taste with salt and pepper. Serve immediately.

John Wayne in *Flame of Barbary Coast* (1945).

DID YOU KNOW?

Largely known for his collaborations with Gene Autry and Roy Rogers, Joseph Kane directed John Wayne in four films: *The Lawless Nineties* (1936), *King of the Pecos* (1936), *The Lonely Trail* (1936) and *Flame of Barbary Coast* (1945).

59

Western WHITE CHICKEN CHILI

THIS RECIPE WILL LEAVE EVEN THE HUNGRIEST AND MOST GRIZZLED OF TRAIL HANDS WITH A FULL BELLY AND A BIG SMILE.

Serves 4-6

PROVISIONS

6 cups chicken stock

4 cups shredded cooked chicken

2 (15-oz.) cans white beans, rinsed and drained

2 cups salsa verde (store bought or see pg. 246)

2 tsp. ground cumin

Kosher salt, to taste

Black pepper, to taste

DIRECTIONS

1. Combine chicken stock, chicken, beans, salsa and cumin in a large stockpot over medium-high heat and bring to a boil. Reduce heat and simmer for 5 minutes or until heated through. Taste and add salt and pepper as needed.

John Wayne and Syd Saylor in *Born to the West* (1937)

DID YOU KNOW? Long before he appeared in *The Three Mesquiteers* (1936), Syd Saylor lost his father in the 1906 San Francisco earthquake, a disaster which Duke survives (as Duke Fergus) in *Flame of Barbary Coast* (1945).

Kickin' Buffalo
Chicken Meatballs,
pg. 78

STARTERS

TURN ANY MEAL INTO A FIESTA WITH
THESE SAVORY SMALL PLATES.

ARTICHOKE DIP

THIS TIME-TESTED APP TURNS ANY MEAL INTO A FANCY AFFAIR WITHOUT THE FRILLS.

Serves 10-12

PROVISIONS

2 (14-oz.) cans artichoke hearts in water, drained

1 medium yellow onion, roughly chopped

2 cloves garlic, roughly chopped

2 cups mayonnaise

2 cups grated Parmesan cheese (6 oz.)

DIRECTIONS

1. Preheat oven to 375 degrees F.

2. Place the drained artichoke hearts in a food processor with the onion and garlic. Pulse several times to chop. Add the mayonnaise and Parmesan cheese and process until almost smooth.

3. Scrape the mixture into a one-quart baking dish and bake 35 minutes or until bubbly and golden brown.

John Wayne and Louise Latimer in *California Straight Ahead!* (1937).

DID YOU KNOW?

California Straight Ahead! (1937) was the first in a series of four Universal films John Wayne made with director Arthur Lubin at the helm, followed by *I Cover the War!* (1937), *Idol of the Crowds* (1937) and *Adventure's End* (1937). Duke's costar, Louise Latimer, later worked with the American Red Cross to promote the war effort.

Bacon-Wrapped DATES

WITH JUST THREE INGREDIENTS, THE ONLY THING THAT'S TOUGH ABOUT THIS RECIPE IS DECIDING WHETHER YOU WANT TO SHARE.

Serves 4

PROVISIONS

16 pitted medjool dates

3 oz. cream cheese

8 slices thin-cut bacon, cut in half

16 toothpicks, soaked in water for 15 minutes

DIRECTIONS

1. Line a rimmed baking sheet with foil or parchment paper. Preheat oven to 350 degrees F.

2. Cut a slit into each date. Spread some cream cheese into the cavity and press the date closed. Wrap with a piece of bacon, insert toothpick to secure and place on the prepared baking sheet. Repeat with the remaining dates.

3. Bake for 15 minutes. Turn the dates over and bake for another 5 to 8 minutes or until the bacon is crispy and browned.

Sophia Loren and John Wayne in *Legend of the Lost* (1957).

Wayne Family Tip

Also called "Devils on Horseback," this recipe tastes just as great with Stilton, cheddar or blue cheese, which will all pack an extra wallop of mouthwatering flavor.

Bacon-Wrapped
JALAPENO POPPERS

HOLD ON TO YOUR HATS—THE HEAT FROM THESE PEPPERS PACKS A PUNCH.

Serves 6

PROVISIONS

12 large jalapeño peppers

4 oz. cream cheese, softened

2 oz. cheddar cheese, grated
(½ cup grated)

8 slices thin-cut bacon

DIRECTIONS

1. Preheat oven to 350 degrees F.

2. Cut peppers in half lengthwise. Scrape out the seeds and veins and discard.

3. Combine the cream and cheddar cheeses in a mixing bowl. Divide the mixture evenly among the pepper halves.

4. Cut the bacon slices into thirds and wrap the peppers, making sure the seam is on the bottom of the pepper. Place in a cast iron skillet or in a baking dish. Bake for 15 to 20 minutes or until the bacon is crisp.

John Wayne lines up for lunch while shooting *The Sons of Katie Elder* (1965).

DID YOU KNOW?

Only four months after having major surgery to remove his left lung and two ribs, John Wayne refused to let his recovery slow him down. He made the gutsy call to perform his own stunts while filming *The Sons of Katie Elder* (1965) and almost caught pneumonia after one scene required him to plunge into a river.

Southern
BACON-WRAPPED SHRIMP

WOW YOUR DINNER CROWD BY SERVING SHRIMP WRAPPED IN BACON, THE KING OF CRISPY MEAT.

Serves 6

PROVISIONS

3 Tbsp. olive oil (divided)

Juice of 1 lemon

Kosher salt, to taste

Black pepper, to taste

24 large shrimp, peeled and deveined

8 slices thin-cut bacon, cut into thirds

24 toothpicks, soaked in water for 15 minutes

4 cups baby arugula

DIRECTIONS

1. Preheat oven to 425 degrees F. Line a rimmed baking sheet with foil and place a cooling rack on top. Place the bacon strips on the rack, leaving some space between each piece, and bake for 5 minutes. Let cool until cool enough to handle.

2. Combine 2 Tbsp. olive oil, juice of ½ lemon and a big pinch of salt and pepper, then pour into a large plastic food storage bag. Add the shrimp and marinate for 10 minutes in the refrigerator. Pat the shrimp dry and discard the marinade.

3. Wrap the bacon pieces around the shrimp and secure with a toothpick. Place on the cooling rack of the prepared pan. Bake for 10 minutes.

4. Toss the arugula with 1 Tbsp. olive oil and the juice from the remaining half of the lemon. Season with salt and pepper and place on a platter. Place the shrimp on top of the arugula and serve.

John Wayne, Ona Munson and Dorothy Dandridge in *Lady from Louisiana* (1941).

John Wayne as Col. John Marlowe in *The Horse Soldiers* (1959). Duke portrayed a colonel seven times over the course of his long career in films like *The Alamo* (1960), *The Green Berets* (1968) and *Rio Lobo* (1970).

Backcountry
BBQ CHICKEN BITES

HOW DO YOU IMPROVE UPON FINGER-LICKIN' PERFECTION? KEEP IT SIMPLE, PILGRIM: JUST ADD BACON.

Serves 7

PROVISIONS

2 boneless, skinless chicken breasts (about 1¾ lbs.)

14 slices thin-cut bacon, cut in half

28 toothpicks, soaked in water for 15 minutes

½ cup barbecue sauce, plus more for serving

DIRECTIONS

1. Preheat oven to 450 degrees F. Line a rimmed baking sheet with foil and place a wire rack on top of the baking sheet.

2. Cut the chicken into 28 bite-sized pieces. Wrap each with a piece of bacon and secure with a toothpick. Place on the wire rack on the prepared baking sheet. Bake for 10 minutes.

3. Carefully remove the baking sheet from the oven and brush each chicken bite with barbecue sauce. Return to the oven for 5 minutes or until the chicken is cooked through and the bacon is crisp.

John Wayne and Oliver Hardy in *The Fighting Kentuckian* (1949).

DID YOU KNOW? After the two performed in John Ford's 1949 stage production of "What Price Glory," Duke personally asked Oliver Hardy if he'd be interested in providing the comic relief in *The Fighting Kentuckian* (1949).

Oven-Baked
REUBEN DIP

TUCK INTO A BOWL OF THIS HEARTY CORNED BEEF DIP THAT TASTES JUST LIKE YOUR FAVORITE SANDWICH.

Serves 10-12

PROVISIONS

Oil for preparing the dish

1 (16-oz.) jar or can sauerkraut, drained and squeezed dry

1 lb. thinly sliced corned beef, chopped

1 lb. Swiss cheese, grated

¾ cup mayonnaise

¾ cup Thousand Island dressing

DIRECTIONS

1. Preheat oven to 350 degrees F. Oil a 9- by 13-inch baking dish.

2. Put all ingredients in a large mixing bowl and stir very well to make sure all ingredients are well combined. Spread the mixture into the prepared baking dish. Bake for 25 minutes or until hot and beginning to brown.

NOTE: This dip is best enjoyed when warm—if possible, serve over a sterno burner or other means of keeping warm.

John Wayne, Gwen Gaze and Don Barclay in *I Cover the War!* (1937).

Wayne Family Tip

Pay homage to this dip's sandwich namesake by serving it with crackers or toasted bread. Or go the extra mile for your guests and bake it into a bread bowl.

Kickin' BUFFALO CHICKEN MEATBALLS

WITH JUST A TOUCH OF HEAT BALANCED BY BLUE CHEESE, THIS SPICY DISH MIGHT CAUSE A STAMPEDE.

Serves 4

PROVISIONS

2 Tbsp. unsalted butter

2 Tbsp. hot sauce (such as Frank's)

12 oz. fully cooked chicken meatballs

2 green onions, thinly sliced

2 oz. crumbled blue cheese

DIRECTIONS

1. In a medium saucepan over medium heat, combine the butter and hot sauce. Cook until the butter is melted. Add the chicken meatballs and cook for 6 to 8 minutes or until the meatballs are heated through. Turn the heat to high and cook for 1 minute, stirring constantly. Let cook for about 5 minutes.

2. Put the meatballs on a platter and sprinkle with the green onions and blue cheese.

Duke in *A Lady Takes a Chance* (1943).

DID YOU KNOW? *A Lady Takes a Chance* (1943) was one of five movies in which John Wayne played a character named Duke, including *Flame of Barbary Coast* (1945) and *Operation Pacific* (1951).

CHIPOTLE BLACK BEAN DIP

THIS FLAVORFUL, EASY-TO-MAKE DIP COMES TOGETHER IN SECONDS AND WORKS HARD SO YOU WON'T HAVE TO.

Serves 4

PROVISIONS

1 (14-oz.) can black beans, drained reserving the liquid and rinsed

1 chipotle pepper in adobo

Juice of 1 lime

1 tsp. ground cumin

¼ tsp. kosher or fine sea salt

¼ tsp. pepper

¼ cup fresh cilantro leaves

DIRECTIONS

1. Place the beans, chipotle pepper, lime juice, cumin, salt and pepper in a blender or food processor. Process until fairly smooth adding some of the reserved bean liquid as needed to get the mixture to a dippable consistency. Taste and add more salt and pepper if needed.

2. Put dip in a serving dish and garnish with cilantro.

John Wayne in a scene from *New Frontier* (1939).

Prospector CRISPY CHICKEN WINGS

HONEY DOES THE TRICK LIKE LIQUID GOLD, CRISPING UP THESE MOUTHWATERING WINGS FOR A MEAL YOUR TASTEBUDS WON'T WANT TO MISS.

Serves 6, approximately 30 wings

PROVISIONS

1 cup barbeque sauce, divided

½ cup honey, divided

4 lbs. chicken wing drumettes

9 oz. crackers

Non-stick cooking spray

DIRECTIONS

1. Pour ¾ cup of the barbeque sauce and ¼ cup of the honey in a large plastic storage bag and mix. Add the chicken wings, close the bag and toss several times to coat the wings with the sauce. Let sit in the refrigerator for at least 30 minutes or up to 24 hours.

2. Preheat oven to 450 degrees F. Spray two baking sheets with non-stick cooking spray.

3. Grind the crackers in a food processor or blender to fine crumbs and pour onto a dinner plate. Remove a chicken wing from the marinade, roll in the cracker crumbs to coat and place on prepared baking sheet. Repeat with remaining chicken wings. Discard the marinade. Spray the tops of the wings lightly with cooking spray. Bake for 25 to 30 minutes or until browned and cooked through (registering 165 degrees F on an instant read thermometer inserted into the thickest part of the wing).

4. Combine the remaining ¼ cup barbecue sauce with the remaining ¼ cup honey and serve with the wings for dipping.

Jim Corey, John Wayne and Harry Woods in *Haunted Gold* (1932).

John Wayne and Capucine in *North to Alaska* (1960). The film opens in Nome, Alaska, the town where Wyatt Earp once opened the two-story Dexter Saloon in 1899. Duke met the fearless lawman while working as a propman.

Gunslinger GUACAMOLE

START YOUR FIESTA OFF WITH A BANG BY WHIPPING UP A GENEROUS BOWL OF THIS TRUSTY SOUTH-OF-THE-BORDER FAVORITE.

Serves 6

PROVISIONS

6 ripe avocados

Juice of 2 limes

10-12 dashes hot sauce, to taste

1 medium red onion, finely chopped

2 Roma tomatoes, seeded and chopped

Kosher salt, to taste

Freshly ground black pepper, to taste

DIRECTIONS

1. Cut the avocados in half, remove the pits and scoop the flesh into a mixing bowl. Mash with a fork or potato masher, leaving some larger chunks of avocado. Stir in the lime juice, hot sauce, onion and tomatoes. Season to taste with salt and pepper.

2. Serve immediately or place the guacamole in a serving bowl and press a piece of plastic wrap directly on the surface of the guacamole to keep it from turning brown.

DID YOU KNOW?

One of John Wayne's fellow "Mesquiteers" in *The Night Riders* (1939), Ray Corrigan, created a movie ranch on land he purchased in California. Called Corriganville, it featured the army fort seen in Duke's film *Fort Apache* (1948).

John Wayne in *The Night Riders* (1939).

JALAPEÑO PECAN CHEESE BALL

THIS CAN'T-MISS CROWD-PLEASER CAN BE MADE AHEAD OF TIME SO YOU CAN KICK BACK AND LET THE GOOD TIMES ROLL.

Serves 12

PROVISIONS

12 oz. cream cheese, softened

2 cups (8-oz.) grated sharp cheddar cheese

1-2 jalapeños, seeded, deveined and finely chopped

1 Tbsp. Worcestershire sauce

¼ tsp. Kosher or fine sea salt

¼ tsp. black pepper

1 cup pecans, finely chopped

DIRECTIONS

1. Combine the cream and cheddar cheeses in the bowl of an electric mixer, preferably fitted with the paddle attachment. Beat until very smooth, scraping down the sides of the bowl as needed. Add the jalapeño, Worcestershire sauce, salt and pepper and mix well.

2. Place a piece of plastic wrap on a flat surface and scrape the cheese mixture onto it. Using the plastic wrap, form the cheese into a large ball.

3. Place the pecans on a plate and roll the cheese ball around, firmly pressing the pecans into the cheese. Reshape the cheese mixture into a ball, wrap in plastic wrap and refrigerate at least 4 hours.

John Wayne in *The Shepherd of the Hills* (1941).

Straight Shootin' BARBECUE MEATBALLS

THE WHOLE FAMILY WILL WANT TO LAY A HAND ON THESE HEARTY BITE-SIZED MEATBALLS, SO BE SURE TO MAKE EXTRA.

Serves 9

PROVISIONS

4 slices bread, crusts removed, bread torn into small pieces

½ cup milk

2 lbs. ground chuck

½ medium white or yellow onion

1 tsp. kosher or fine sea salt

½ tsp. black pepper

1 (18-oz.) bottle barbecue sauce

DIRECTIONS

1. Preheat oven to 375 degrees F.

2. Place the torn bread into a large mixing bowl and pour the milk over it. Let sit for 5 to 10 minutes. Add the ground chuck. Using the large holes of a box grater, grate the onion into the bowl. Add the salt and pepper. Mix to combine well. Shape into 1-inch balls and place on a rimmed baking sheet or in a 9- by 13-inch baking dish. Bake for 25 minutes. Leave the oven on.

3. Drain any grease from the baking pan. Pour the barbecue sauce over the meatballs and gently toss to coat. Return the meatballs to the oven for another 10 minutes or until cooked through. Serve warm. (Can be made ahead and stored, covered, in the refrigerator. Reheat at 350 degress F for about 10 minutes.)

John Wayne in *The Shootist* (1976).

Pacific Coast
SMOKED SALMON DIP

IF YOU AND YOURS SHARE DUKE'S LOVE OF THE SEA, THIS SAVORY STARTER WILL MAKE WAVES AT YOUR NEXT FAMILY GET-TOGETHER.

Serves 4

PROVISIONS

8 oz. cream cheese, softened

⅓ cup sour cream

Juice of 1 lemon (2 Tbsp.)

3 oz. smoked salmon, chopped

¼ cup fresh dill,
measured then minced

½ tsp. kosher or fine sea salt

¼ tsp. black pepper

DIRECTIONS

1. Beat the cream cheese, sour cream and lemon juice together. Beat in the smoked salmon, dill, salt and pepper. Put into a bowl and cover with plastic wrap. Refrigerate until serving time.

Duke enjoys a bit of deep sea fishing in the Pacifi

DID YOU KNOW?

A body surfer in his younger days, Duke never lost his love for the open water and especially enjoyed sport fishing off the Gulf of California. His beloved boat, the *Wild Goose*, was placed on the National Register of Historic Places in 2011 and can still be seen in Newport Beach, California.

Pear & Cranberry
Stuffed Pork
Chops, pg. 126

MAINS

THESE HEARTY HELPINGS WILL KEEP THE WHOLE FAMILY SMILING.

Baked
SALT & VINEGAR COD

KETTLE CHIPS ARE THE KEY TO A CRUNCHY, FLAKY COD FILLET IN THIS ALL-AMERICAN TAKE ON FISH AND CHIPS. BRING A TASTE OF THE SEA RIGHT TO YOUR TABLE.

Serves 4

PROVISIONS

4 (4-oz.) cod fillets

Kosher or fine sea salt, to taste

Freshly ground black pepper, to taste

2 tsp. mayonnaise

1 (2-oz.) bag kettle cooked salt and vinegar potato chips, crushed (about 2½ cups)

Tartar sauce, for serving

DIRECTIONS

1. Preheat oven to 400 degrees F and line a baking sheet with parchment paper or a silicone baking mat.

2. Arrange the fish fillets on the prepared baking sheet and sprinkle with a small pinch of salt and a large pinch of pepper, then brush each fillet with ½ tsp. mayonnaise.

Top the fish fillets with the crushed potato chips, gently pressing down to coat the fillets. Bake for 10 minutes or until the fish flakes easily with a fork.

3. Serve with Tartar sauce.

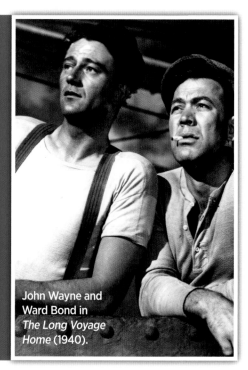

DID YOU KNOW?

As lifelong friends and collaborators, John Wayne and Ward Bond appeared in more than 20 films together over the course of their long careers. Some of Bond's most notable Duke-free credits include *Gone With the Wind* (1939), *The Maltese Falcon* (1941) and *It's a Wonderful Life* (1946).

John Wayne and Ward Bond in *The Long Voyage Home* (1940).

Wayne Family Tip

This dish pairs well with a heaping side of coleslaw, baked beans, hush puppies or succotash. For authentic pub food fare, look no further than roasted potato wedges or mushy peas.

Wayne Family Tip

Turn up the heat on long winter nights by incorporating spicy Italian sausage into the mix. Or switch things up by adding savory bratwurst, smoky kielbasa or turkey sausage.

Barbary Coast
BAKED SAUSAGE & BEANS

STACK THE DECK IN YOUR FAVOR BY DEALING OUT HEAPING PLATEFULS OF THIS NO MUSS, NO FUSS MEAL TO YOUR HUNGRY CREW—THEY'LL BE SURE TO THANK YOU.

Serves 6

PROVISIONS

3 Tbsp. olive oil,
plus more for preparing the pan

8 slices multigrain bread

2 pt. cherry or grape tomatoes, halved

2 (15.5-oz.) cans cannellini beans, undrained

2 Tbsp. balsamic
or red wine vinegar

2 tsp. kosher or fine sea salt

1 tsp. freshly ground black pepper

1 tsp. Italian seasoning

12 oz. little pork sausages

DIRECTIONS

1. Preheat oven to 350 degrees F. Brush a 9- by 13-inch (or similar) baking dish with olive oil.

2. Cut the bread into 1-inch cubes and place in the prepared baking dish with the tomatoes.

3. Pour the beans and their liquid into a mixing bowl. Add 3 Tbsp. olive oil, vinegar, salt, pepper and Italian seasoning, stirring well, then add to the bread mixture. Nestle the sausages into the bread and bake for 45 minutes.

Ann Dvorak and Duke in *Flame of Barbary Coast* (1945).

Roaming Buffalo ROASTED CHICKEN

THE SMELL OF THIS ZESTY OVEN-ROASTED CHICKEN WAFTING THROUGH YOUR KITCHEN WILL ENTICE EVEN THE FEISTIEST TRAIL HANDS EVERY TIME.

Serves 6

PROVISIONS

1 (4-lb.) whole chicken

Kosher or fine sea salt, to taste

Garlic powder, for seasoning

Black pepper, for seasoning

1 lemon, cut into quarters

3 Tbsp. butter

2 Tbsp. hot sauce (such as Frank's)

DIRECTIONS

1. Preheat oven to 450 degrees F.

2. Remove anything from the inside of the chicken and pat dry all over. Season the cavity and outside of the chicken generously with salt, garlic powder and pepper. Stuff the lemon wedges into the cavity. Roast for 45 minutes or until the juices run clear. Remove from oven.

3. Melt the butter and hot sauce together in a small saucepan. Brush the chicken all over with the sauce. Let rest for 15 minutes. Remove the lemon wedges from the cavity and serve.

John Wayne and Jeffrey Hunter in *The Searchers* (1956).

CHICKEN FETTUCCINE ALFREDO

NOTHING BEATS THE PRIDE (OR LINGERING HEAVENLY AROMA) THAT COMES WITH COOKING THIS ITALIAN FAVORITE.

Serves 6

PROVISIONS

Kosher or fine sea salt, to taste

1 lb. fettuccine

4 Tbsp. unsalted butter

2 cups heavy cream

2 cups shredded cooked chicken

1¼ cups grated Parmesan cheese, plus more for serving

Freshly ground black pepper, to taste

DIRECTIONS

1. Bring a pot of salted water to a boil. Cook the fettuccine according to the package directions. Reserve 2 cups of the cooking water, then drain the pasta and rinse with hot water.

2. Heat the butter in a large skillet over medium heat. Add the cream and ½ cup of the pasta water. Bring to a simmer. Add the fettuccine, chicken and Parmesan cheese, then toss to coat. Season to taste with salt and pepper. If the pasta is dry, add more of the pasta cooking water a little at a time.

3. Sprinkle additional Parmesan on top and serve immediately.

DID YOU KNOW?

When making *Legend of the Lost* (1957), Batjac Productions spent 12 weeks filming exterior shots at Cinecittà Studios in Rome, Italy. Duke returned to Cinecittà to complete filming on *Cast a Giant Shadow* (1966).

Duke prepares to dig in at Rome's Il Vero Alfredo Restaurant.

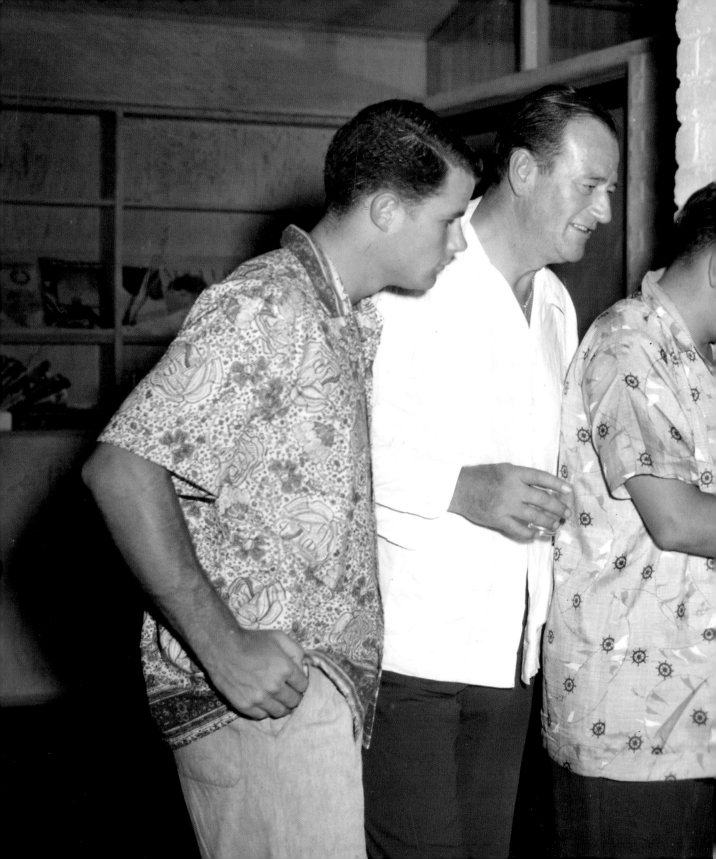

Duke checks in on his dinner. For as much as the actor enjoyed partaking in a good meal, what really mattered most to him was gathering around the table with his friends and family to enjoy each other's company.

CHICKEN PARMESAN PASTA SUPREME

ON A DAY WHEN SALAD JUST WON'T CUT IT, BRING OUT THE BIG GUNS WITH A FLAVOR-LOADED AND FILLING MEAL THAT WON'T BACK DOWN.

Serves 4

PROVISIONS

12 oz. fusilli or penne

1 rotisserie chicken

1 Tbsp. minced fresh rosemary

1 cup grated Parmesan cheese, divided

½ tsp. kosher or fine sea salt

½ tsp. freshly ground black pepper

Olive oil, for serving

DIRECTIONS

1. Bring a large pot of heavily salted water to a boil, add the pasta and cook according to the package directions. Reserve 1 cup of the starchy cooking water, drain the pasta, then return the pasta to the pot.

2. While the pasta is cooking, shred the chicken, discarding the skin and bones. Add the chicken to the drained pasta with the reserved starchy cooking water, rosemary, ¾ cup Parmesan cheese, salt and pepper. Cook, stirring, over medium-low until the sauce thickens slightly, 3 to 4 minutes.

3. To serve, drizzle with some olive oil and sprinkle with the remaining ¼ cup Parmesan cheese.

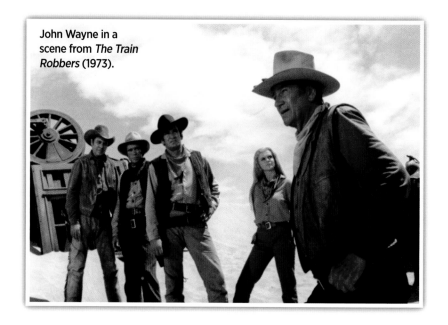

John Wayne in a scene from *The Train Robbers* (1973).

Wayne Family Tip

Add more texture to this dish by opting for medium-grind cornmeal. These chicken tenders also taste great served with a side of Buttermilk Chive Ranch Dressing (see pg. 228).

Homestyle
CORNMEAL-CRUSTED CHICKEN TENDERS

THE CRUNCHY CORNMEAL BREADING ON THESE TASTY MORSELS WILL TAKE YOU BACK TO A SIMPLER TIME.

Serves 4

PROVISIONS

- 1 lb. chicken tenders
- Kosher or fine sea salt, to taste
- Black pepper, to taste
- ½ cup cornmeal
- 2 tsp. Cajun seasoning
- 1 large egg
- 1 Tbsp. water
- 2 Tbsp. vegetable or olive oil
- Barbecue sauce

DIRECTIONS

1. Season the chicken tenders with salt and pepper. In a shallow bowl, combine the cornmeal with the Cajun seasoning and a pinch of salt and pepper. In another bowl, beat the egg with 1 Tbsp. water and a small pinch of salt. Have an empty plate standing by.

2. Dip the chicken tenders first into the egg then into the cornmeal, pressing the cornmeal into the chicken. Place on the clean plate.

3. In a large non-stick skillet, heat the oil over medium-high until it begins to shimmer. Turn the heat down to medium and add the chicken tenders. Cook for 3 minutes then flip and cook for another 4 to 5 minutes or until golden brown and the internal temperature of the chicken reaches 165 degrees F.

4. Serve with the barbecue sauce for dipping.

Duke (left) smiles with his family and beloved dog, Duke.

Knockout
CRISPY PORK CHOPS

CRISP UP AN OLD STANDARD AND YOUR LOVED ONES WILL BE RARIN' TO THROW DOWN OVER WHO GETS DIBS ON SECONDS.

— *Serves 8* —

PROVISIONS

8 thin-cut bone-in pork chops

1 cup flour

1 tsp. kosher or fine sea salt

1 tsp. pepper

1 tsp. garlic powder

1 tsp. paprika

½ cup vegetable oil

2 Tbsp. butter

DIRECTIONS

1. Dry the pork chops well with paper towels. Combine the flour, salt, pepper, garlic powder and paprika on a plate and mix well. Dredge the pork chops in the flour mixture and place on a clean plate. Let sit for 2 to 3 minutes then dredge them in the flour mixture one more time.

2. Heat the oil in a large cast iron skillet over medium-high heat. Add the butter and let it melt. Fry 2 to 3 pork chops at a time for 3 to 4 minutes or until golden brown.

3. Flip and fry on the other side for 2 minutes or until golden brown and no pink juices remain. Keep warm while frying the rest of the pork chops.

DID YOU KNOW?

Like his good friend Duke, Ward Bond also played football for the University of Southern California. The two former teammates forged an enduring kinship after director John Ford hired them to appear in his 1929 film *Salute*.

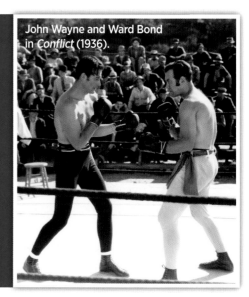

John Wayne and Ward Bond in *Conflict* (1936).

Wayne Family Tip

You can make this beef brisket up to 3 days in advance. Just salt the meat, cover it tightly in plastic wrap, and place it in the fridge until you're ready to get cooking.

Wayne Family Tip

Adding a pinch or two of brown sugar to your flour mixture will make for an even crispier pork chop with just a hint of caramelized sweetness.

Easy-to-Make
BEEF BRISKET

EVEN THE RUSTIEST CHEF CAN HOP BACK IN THE SADDLE BY DISHING OUT THIS BRISKET LIKE NOBODY'S BUSINESS.

Serves 4

PROVISIONS

1 (3-lb.) beef brisket, trimmed of fat

1 tsp. kosher salt

½ tsp. black pepper

1 large white or yellow onion, thinly sliced

12 oz. barbecue sauce

1½ cups water

1 (10-oz.) can diced tomatoes and chilies, undrained

1½ lb. small white potatoes

DIRECTIONS

1. Preheat oven to 325 degrees F.

2. Combine the salt and pepper in a small bowl and rub all over the brisket. Place in a baking dish. Cover the beef with the sliced onions.

3. Combine the barbecue sauce, water, canned tomatoes and chilies, then pour over the beef. Cover the dish with foil and bake for 3 hours. Leave the oven on.

4. Remove the foil, add the potatoes and cook uncovered for another 40 to 45 minutes or until the potatoes are tender. Let rest for 10 minutes, then slice the beef and return to the dish. Spoon the sauce over the beef and serve.

DID YOU KNOW?

When contractual obligations forced director John Farrow to leave the set of *Hondo* (1953) to begin working on another film, Duke's old friend John Ford stepped in to wrap up the last few scenes. He took no credit.

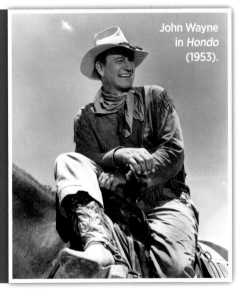

John Wayne in *Hondo* (1953).

Bullseye BABY BACK RIBS

THESE FALL-OFF-THE-BONE BARBECUE RIBS NEVER MISS THE MARK.

Serves 6

PROVISIONS

2 racks pork baby back ribs

¾ cup Rocky Mountain Barbecue Seasoning (see pg. 224)

½ cup barbecue sauce

DIRECTIONS

1. Flip the ribs bone side up. Insert a dinner knife just under the white membrane covering the meat and bones, then gently peel off the membrane.

2. Coat the ribs on both sides generously with the barbecue seasoning and bring to room temperature.

3. Preheat the oven to 250 degrees F.

4. Wrap each rack of ribs with foil and place on a baking sheet. Cook for 2½ to 3 hours or until the ribs are tender. Remove the ribs from the oven and set the oven to broil with the top rack about 6 inches from the heat source.

5. Remove the ribs from the foil and place on the baking sheet. Brush both sides with barbecue sauce and broil for about 4 minutes per side.

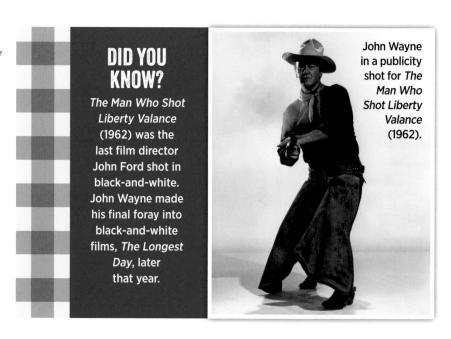

DID YOU KNOW?

The Man Who Shot Liberty Valance (1962) was the last film director John Ford shot in black-and-white. John Wayne made his final foray into black-and-white films, *The Longest Day*, later that year.

John Wayne in a publicity shot for *The Man Who Shot Liberty Valance* (1962).

Wayne Family Tip

When the chicken is finished, be sure to avoid the urge to soak up the grease with paper towels. This can actually make the nice crispy finish turn soggy— and no one wants that!

Finger-Lickin' FRIED CHICKEN

BRING A PLATTER OF THIS BELOVED SOUTHERN STAPLE TO YOUR NEXT HOOTENANNY AND WATCH YOUR NEIGHBORS HOLLER FOR MORE.

Serves 4-5

PROVISIONS

3 cups buttermilk

1 Tbsp. plus 2 tsp. kosher or fine sea salt, divided

1 tsp. hot sauce

1 whole fryer chicken, cut into 10 pieces

2 cups flour

2 Tbsp. paprika

2 tsp. black pepper

Vegetable oil

DIRECTIONS

Start this recipe the night before or early in the day you plan to serve the chicken. Note: An instant-read thermometer is useful not only for keeping the oil temperature correct, but for checking the doneness of the chicken.

1. In a large mixing bowl, large enough to hold all the chicken, combine the buttermilk with 1 Tbsp. salt and hot sauce. Add the chicken, stirring to coat, then cover the bowl with plastic wrap and refrigerate 8 to 24 hours.

2. Drain the chicken in a colander.

3. In a large paper bag, combine the flour, paprika, 2 tsp. salt and 2 tsp. pepper and shake to mix well.

4. Add the chicken (do not dry off the buttermilk) to the bag a few pieces at a time and shake vigorously to coat. Place the chicken on a board or plate and let sit while the oil heats up.

5. Place a wire cooling rack over a sheet pan.

6. Put a large skillet on the stove over medium heat. Add enough vegetable oil to come up ½ inch on the skillet. Heat the oil to 325 degrees F. Fry the chicken in batches, making sure not to overcrowd the pan, until golden brown on both sides and the chicken has an internal temperature of 165 degrees F, about 7 to 12 minutes per side depending on size. As the chicken pieces get done, place them on the wire rack to drain and sprinkle with a pinch of salt while still hot. Make sure the oil temperature does not go above 325 degrees F or below 300 degrees F. Keep adjusting the heat as needed.

GARLIC ROASTED CHICKEN
and Frontier Potatoes

THIS OVEN-ROASTED CHICKEN DELIVERS A SPICY KICK THAT'LL PUT THE PEP BACK IN YOUR STEP.

— *Serves 4* —

PROVISIONS

2 lb. small Yukon gold potatoes

3 Tbsp. olive oil, divided

1 tsp. kosher or fine sea salt

1 tsp. black pepper

4 garlic cloves, minced

Juice of 1 lemon (2 Tbsp.)

⅛ tsp. red pepper flakes

4 boneless, skinless chicken breasts

DIRECTIONS

1. Position oven rack in lower third of the oven and preheat oven to 425 degrees F. Toss potatoes with 1 Tbsp. oil, salt and pepper. Spread into an even layer on a rimmed baking sheet and roast until the potatoes begin to brown, 25 to 30 minutes.

2. Heat 2 Tbsp. olive oil in a small skillet over medium heat. Add the garlic and cook, stirring, until fragrant, about 30 seconds (do not brown the garlic). Remove from heat and add the lemon juice and red pepper flakes.

3. Season the chicken breasts on both sides with salt and pepper. Remove the baking sheet from the oven and push the potatoes to the sides. Place the chicken breasts in the middle of the pan and drizzle with the garlic mixture. Return to the oven and cook until the chicken is cooked through and the potatoes are tender, about 20 minutes.

DID YOU KNOW?

Before co-starring with John Wayne in *The Lawless Frontier* (1934) and *Haunted Gold* (1932), pre-Code starlet Sheila Terry shared the screen with Humphrey Bogart in *Big City Blues* (1932) and *Three on a Match* (1932).

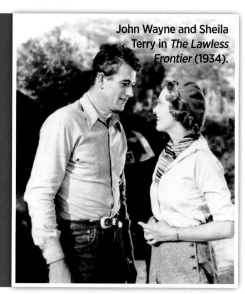

John Wayne and Sheila Terry in *The Lawless Frontier* (1934).

Wayne Family Tip

Feeding an especially hungry crowd? Serve this dish with generous platefuls of glazed carrots, roasted green beans or a colorful medley of steamed vegetables.

Victor McLaglen, Maureen O'Hara and John Wayne in *The Quiet Man* (1952). Four of Duke's children—Patrick, Melinda, Toni and Michael—appeared onscreen in the film's horse race scene, which was filmed in Connemara, Ireland.

Irish LAMB CHOPS WITH POTATOES AND PEAS

SIMPLE AND SATISFYING, THIS WHOLESOME RECIPE HARKENS BACK TO THE JOYS OF COUNTRY LIVING ON THE EMERALD ISLE.

Serves 2

PROVISIONS

4 lamb chops (about 1-inch thick)

Kosher or fine sea salt, to taste

Black pepper, to taste

2 large gold potatoes

2–3 Tbsp. olive oil

3 rosemary sprigs

2 cups frozen baby peas, unthawed

¼ cup chopped fresh mint

DIRECTIONS

1. Season the lamb chops on both sides with salt and pepper and let sit at room temperature while the potatoes cook.

2. Wash the potatoes and cut into ½ inch cubes. Place in a large skillet over high heat and cover with boiling water and 1 tsp. salt. When the water returns to a boil, cook for 10 minutes or until the potatoes are fork tender. Drain the potatoes into a colander and return the pan to the heat. Add 2 Tbsp. of oil to the pan and let it get hot.

3. When the oil is hot, add the lamb chops and cook for 2 minutes per side. Remove from the pan and place on a clean plate. Add the drained potatoes back to the pan, if needed add another Tbsp. of oil, lower the heat to medium-high and let cook, undisturbed for 1 minute. Flip the potatoes, add the lamb back to the pan, nestling among the potatoes, add the rosemary and peas and let cook for another 2 minutes or until the peas are heated through and the lamb reaches 145 degrees F on an instant read thermometer (for medium rare). Sprinkle the mint over the top and serve.

Pistachio Mint Crusted
RACK OF LAMB

THIS TENDER AND TASTY MEAL WILL FILL YOUR STOMACH AND WARM YOUR HEART.

Serves 6

PROVISIONS

2 (8 bones each) racks of lamb, trimmed and frenched

Kosher salt and black pepper, to taste

3 Tbsp. olive oil, use divided

½ cup shelled, roasted, salted pistachios

3 cups mint leaves

3 cloves garlic, minced

Zest and juice of 1 lemon

DIRECTIONS

1. Preheat oven to 450 degrees F.

2. Heat an oven proof skillet large enough to hold both racks of lamb until hot over medium-high. If you do not have a skillet large enough for both racks, place a roasting pan in the oven to heat as the oven does.

3. Season the lamb generously with salt and pepper on all sides. Heat 1 Tbsp. of oil in the pan and sear the lamb on all sides for about 2 minutes per side. Let the lamb cool a little.

4. Put the pistachios in the bowl of a food processor and pulse a few times to grind them. Add the remaining 2 Tbsp. of olive oil, mint, garlic, zest and juice of the lemon and process until it turns into a paste. Spread the paste on the meat-side of the lamb racks, pressing down firmly, then place the lamb racks back in the skillet (or in a roasting pan) bone-side down. Roast for 20 minutes for medium rare, 25 minutes for medium. Cover the lamb with a piece of foil and let rest for 10 minutes. Use a sharp, thin knife to carve the lamb into chops. Serve.

John Wayne and Joan Blondell in *Lady for a Night* (1942).

Pear & Cranberry STUFFED PORK CHOPS

NO NEED TO WAIT UNTIL NOVEMBER TO COOK UP THESE THANKSGIVING-INSPIRED PORK CHOPS. SWEET PEAR AND TART CRANBERRY LIVEN UP THIS MEAL FOR A PERFECT PAIRING THAT'LL MAKE YOUR TASTEBUDS GRATEFUL.

Serves 4

PROVISIONS

4 thick boneless pork chops

1 bunch green onions

1 tsp. poultry seasoning

1½ tsp. kosher or fine sea salt

½ tsp. freshly ground black pepper

1 Tbsp. olive oil, plus more for brushing

2 firm but ripe pears, peeled, cored and diced into ¼-inch cubes

½ cup dried cranberries

DIRECTIONS

1. Preheat oven to 350 degrees F.

2. Butterfly the pork chops and pat dry with paper towels. Slice the white and light green parts of the green onions and mince the green tops. Combine the poultry seasoning with the salt and pepper.

3. In a large, oven-proof skillet, heat 1 Tbsp. olive oil over medium-high. Add the white and light green parts of the green onions and sauté for 1 minute. Add the pears, cranberries and 1 tsp. of the poultry seasoning mixture and cook, stirring often, until the pears are tender and start to brown, about 8 minutes. Transfer the mixture to a bowl and wash and dry the skillet.

4. Sprinkle half the remaining poultry seasoning mixture on the insides of the pork chops and rub it in well. Spoon a heaping Tbsp. of the pear mixture into the center of each pork chop, then close and secure the openings with toothpicks. You will have a little over half the pear mixture leftover—reserve this for later. Brush both sides of the pork chops with olive oil and season with the remaining poultry seasoning mixture.

5. Heat the skillet over medium-high heat. Add the pork chops and sear for 2 to 3 minutes. Flip and sear the other side for 1 to 2 minutes. Place the skillet in the oven and cook for 20 to 25 minutes or until an instant read thermometer inserted into the meat (not the stuffing) reads 160 degrees F. Transfer the pork chops to a serving platter. Put the skillet (along with any juices that have accumulated during cooking) on the stove over medium-high heat.

6. Add the reserved pear mixture and cook for 1 minute, stirring to coat the mixture with the pan juices. Take off the heat and stir in the minced green onion tops. Remove the toothpicks from the chops, spoon the pear mixture on top, and serve.

Maple Mustard ROASTED SALMON

AN AVID FISHERMAN, DUKE KNEW DINNER TASTES BETTER WHEN YOU'VE CAUGHT IT WITH YOUR OWN TWO HANDS.

Serves 4

PROVISIONS

4 (5-oz.) salmon fillets

Kosher or fine sea salt, to taste

Black pepper, to taste

2 Tbsp. mayonnaise

2 Tbsp. maple syrup

2 Tbsp. Dijon mustard

¼ cup chopped parsley

DIRECTIONS

1. Preheat oven to 400 degrees F. Line a baking sheet with foil or parchment paper.

2. Season the salmon with salt and pepper. Combine the mayonnaise, maple syrup and mustard in a small bowl, stirring until smooth. Place the salmon fillets on the prepared baking sheet, skin side down. Spread the maple mustard sauce over the top of the salmon and bake for 8 minutes. Remove from the oven, turn on the broiler, and broil for 2 minutes.

3. Sprinkle with the parsley and serve.

Duke, Pilar and friends hang out on the open water.

DID YOU KNOW?

Whenever he wasn't filming, Duke loved to sail with friends and family to destinations as varied as the waters around Mexico to the Pacific Northwest. The Wayne family also had a special fondness for Catalina Island.

Pan-Seared PORK ROAST WITH CIDER GRAVY

DRESS UP YOUR PORK ROAST WITH THIS CAN'T-MISS CIDER GRAVY FOR A MOUTHWATERING MEAL THAT'S SURE TO PLEASE.

Serves 4-6

PROVISIONS

2 Tbsp. olive oil

1 (2½-lb.) boneless pork roast, trimmed and tied

Kosher or fine sea salt and freshly ground black pepper, to taste

1 medium white or yellow onion, peeled and sliced

1 medium apple, cored and sliced

1 medium pear, cored and sliced

12 oz. apple cider

DIRECTIONS

1. Preheat oven to 375 degrees F.

2. In a Dutch oven or oven-proof covered pan, heat the oil over medium. Season the pork on all sides generously with salt and pepper. Brown the pork on all sides, about 4 minutes per side. Remove the pork from the pan and set aside.

3. Add the onion, apple and pear to the pan. Season with a large pinch of salt and pepper. Cook until soft and beginning to brown, about 8 minutes. Pour in the cider, scraping the pan to release any of the brown bits at the bottom of the pan. Add the pork back into the pan. Cover and bake in the oven until the pork registers 145 degrees F on an instant read thermometer, about 40 minutes.

Duke in *Allegheny Uprising* (1939).

Homesteader's OVEN-BAKED CHICKEN

YOU PROBABLY ALREADY HAVE THESE HANDY PROVISIONS IN YOUR FRIDGE RIGHT NOW, SO DO YOURSELF A FAVOR AND GET COOKIN'!

Serves 4

PROVISIONS

Vegetable oil for preparing the baking dish

4 boneless, skinless chicken breasts

Kosher or fine sea salt, to taste

Black pepper, to taste

½ cup barbecue sauce

2 slices thick-cut bacon

4 oz. grated sharp cheddar cheese (1 cup grated)

DIRECTIONS

1. Preheat oven to 400 degrees F. Brush a 9- by 12-inch baking dish with oil.

2. Season both sides of the chicken breasts with salt and pepper. Place in the prepared baking dish and brush both sides liberally with the barbecue sauce. Cover with foil and bake for 40 minutes.

3. Chop the bacon into small pieces and place in a cold frying pan. Turn the heat to medium and cook, stirring occasionally, until mostly crispy. Drain on a paper towel.

4. After 40 minutes, remove the foil from the chicken, top with grated cheese and bacon, and bake for another 5 to 10 minutes or until the chicken registers 165 degrees F on an instant read thermometer and the cheese is melted and the bacon crispy.

DID YOU KNOW?

Before he acquired the 26 Bar Ranch, Duke appreciated the natural beauty of Arizona while filming a slew of movies, including *The Big Trail* (1930), *Stagecoach* (1939), *Angel and the Badman* (1947) and *Red River* (1948).

John Wayne on his 26 Bar Ranch.

Wayne Family Tip

If you'd rather not crumble your sausage, serve it sliced for extra presentation. Add a pinch of crushed fennel seeds to give this dish an irresistible aroma.

SAUSAGE & KALE PASTA

IF YOU'RE FIXING FOR GREENS BUT ARE FRESH OUT OF COLLARDS, THIS DOWNHOME DISH WILL GO THE EXTRA MILE.

Serves 4

PROVISIONS

1 Tbsp. olive oil

1 lb. sweet or spicy Italian sausage, casings removed and crumbled

10 cups chopped kale

1 tsp. kosher salt, plus more for seasoning

½ tsp. black pepper, plus more for seasoning

2 Tbsp. balsamic vinegar

8 oz. linguine or other pasta

½ cup grated Parmesan cheese

DIRECTIONS

1. Heat olive oil in a large skillet over medium-high. Add the sausage and cook until the sausage is no longer pink, 3 to 4 minutes. Drain off all but 1 Tbsp. of the fat.

2. Add the kale, salt and black pepper. Reduce heat to medium-low, cover the pan and cook for 20 minutes or until the kale is tender. Increase heat to high, add the balsamic vinegar and cook, stirring, until the vinegar is evaporated. Remove from the heat.

3. While the sauce is cooking, bring a large pot of heavily salted water to a boil. Cook the linguine according to the package directions. Reserve ½ cup of the pasta cooking water, drain the pasta, rinse with hot water and add to the pan with the sausage and kale along with ¼ cup of the reserved pasta water. Stir to combine, adding a little more pasta water if the dish seems dry. Adjust seasoning with more salt and pepper if desired.

4. Serve with Parmesan cheese.

DID YOU KNOW?

Henry Fonda teamed up with Duke's longtime director and friend John Ford to make a total of nine films, including *Young Mr. Lincoln* (1939), *The Grapes of Wrath* (1940), *The Fugitive* (1947) and *Mister Roberts* (1955).

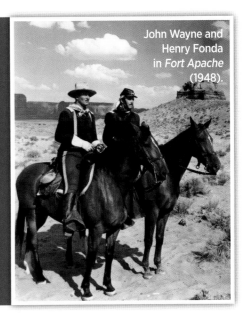

John Wayne and Henry Fonda in *Fort Apache* (1948).

SAUSAGE AND APPLE BAKE

GOOD THINGS TAKE TIME (OR IN THIS CASE THYME), BUT YOU'LL KNOW YOU MADE THE RIGHT CALL AFTER JUST ONE BITE OF THIS SAVORY BAKE.

Serves 4

PROVISIONS

- 1½ lb. small fingerling potatoes
- 1½ lb. baby carrots
- 2 large tart apples, cut into 1-inch cubes
- 1 tsp. dried thyme
- 1 tsp. kosher or fine sea salt
- ½ tsp. black pepper
- 4 Tbsp. olive oil, divided
- 4 turkey or Italian sausages in casings

DIRECTIONS

1. Preheat oven to 400 degrees F.

2. If some of the potatoes are larger than others, cut in half so they are roughly the same size. Place on a rimmed baking sheet. Add the carrots and apples, drizzle with 3 Tbsp. olive oil and add the thyme, salt and pepper. Toss well, making sure everything is coated with oil.

3. Using a fork, prick the casings of the sausages. Place on top of the vegetables and apples and bake for 40 minutes or until the vegetables are tender and the sausages are cooked through. Turn the broiler to high and broil for about 2 minutes or until the sausages are brown. Drizzle with 1 Tbsp. olive oil before serving.

DID YOU KNOW?

The Horse Soldiers (1959) is loosely based on a cavalry raid that took place in Mississippi during the Civil War. Duke's character, Colonel John Marlowe, is modeled after the real-life Colonel Benjamin Grierson.

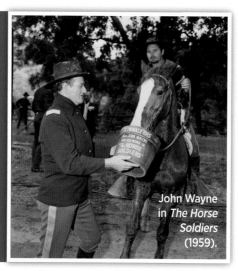

John Wayne in *The Horse Soldiers* (1959).

Stagecoach
SHRIMP SCAMPI

FIVE MINUTES IS ALL IT TAKES TO SERVE UP THIS ZESTY SHRIMP FAVORITE FOR A KNOCKOUT MEAL THAT'S SURE TO IMPRESS.

Serves 4

PROVISIONS

1½ lb. large shrimp, peeled, deveined, tails on or off

½ tsp. kosher or fine sea salt

¼ tsp. black pepper

1 Tbsp. vegetable or olive oil

4 Tbsp. butter, use divided

4 cloves garlic, minced

Juice of 2 lemons (4 Tbsp.)

½ cup chopped parsley

DIRECTIONS

1. Season the shrimp with salt and pepper.

2. Heat the oil and 2 Tbsp. butter in a large skillet over medium-high until the butter melts. Add the garlic and cook, stirring, for 30 seconds.

3. Add the shrimp and cook for 3 minutes, flipping the shrimp halfway through. Add the lemon juice and remaining butter and cook just until the shrimp is opaque, about 2 more minutes. Do not overcook. Remove from heat and stir in the parsley.

4. Serve immediately.

John Wayne in *Stagecoach* (1939).

John Wayne, Charles Coburn and Sigrid Gurie in *Three Faces West* (1940). The film was made under the working title *The Refugee*. Coburn would later costar with Duke as Father Burke in *Trouble Along the Way* (1953).

Campfire Skillet
BBQ BEEF & PEPPERS

YOU WON'T NEED A DINNER BELL TO CORRAL YOUR CLAN WHEN THEY CATCH A WHIFF OF THIS PEPPERY MEAL.

— *Serves 6* —

PROVISIONS

- 1½ lb. flank steak
- Kosher or fine sea salt, to taste
- Black pepper, to taste
- 1 Tbsp. vegetable oil
- 2 bell peppers, seeded, deveined and thinly sliced
- 1 large yellow or white onion, cut into 12 wedges
- ¾ cup barbecue sauce

DIRECTIONS

1. Cut the flank steak across the grain into ¼-inch strips. Season generously with salt and pepper.

2. Heat the oil in a large skillet over medium-high. Add the steak and cook, stirring frequently, until it is browned, about 5 to 6 minutes. Remove from the skillet and transfer to a plate.

3. Stir in the peppers and onions and cook until they are crisp-tender, about 4 minutes. Add the beef and barbecue sauce to the skillet and cook, stirring occasionally, until heated through, 2 to 3 minutes.

DID YOU KNOW?

After more than 30 years of starring in movies, John Wayne took home a hard-earned, well-deserved Academy Award for his portrayal of U.S. Marshal Rooster Cogburn in the 1969 classic *True Grit*.

Duke in *True Grit* (1969).

Slow Cooked Rustic
MUSTARD ROAST

PATIENCE MIGHT BE A VIRTUE WHEN COOKING THIS DISH. BUT DON'T LET THAT STOP YOU FROM GOBBLING DOWN EVERY LAST BITE.

Serves 4

PROVISIONS

¼ **cup olive oil**

¼ **cup Dijon mustard**

2 **tsp. dried thyme**

2 **tsp. kosher or fine sea salt**

1 **tsp. black pepper**

1 **(4-lb.) chuck roast**

1 **cup beef broth**

2 **Tbsp. flour**

DIRECTIONS

1. Combine the oil, mustard, thyme, salt and pepper in a small bowl. Place the roast in a slow cooker and brush the mustard mixture all over the roast. Pour in the beef broth and cook on low for 8 hours or high for 4 hours.

2. Pour the liquid out of the slow cooker into a liquid measuring cup or pitcher. Let sit for a few minutes to allow the fat to rise to the top. Spoon 2 Tbsp. of the fat into a large skillet and heat on medium. Spoon off most of the rest of the fat.

3. Add the flour to the oil in the pan and cook, stirring, for 1 minute. Pour in the reserved liquid and cook, stirring occasionally, until thickened, about 5 minutes.

4. Serve the gravy with the roast.

Ricky Nelson, John Wayne and Dean Martin in *Rio Bravo* (1959).

145

Slow Cooker
PORK ROAST AND POTATOES

WHEN THERE'S A DAY CHOCK-FULL OF ADVENTURE AHEAD OF YOU, PUT THE WHOLE DARN PORK ROAST IN THE SLOW COOKER FOR A FILLING MEAL THAT'LL BE READY WHEN YOU ARE.

Serves 6-8

PROVISIONS

1 (1 ½-2 lb.) boneless pork roast

Kosher or fine sea salt, to taste

Black pepper, to taste

1½–2 lb. red potatoes, cut into halves or quarters

12 garlic cloves, peeled and left whole

1 cup beef or chicken broth

2 tsp. Italian seasoning

DIRECTIONS

1. Season the pork with salt and pepper and place in the slow cooker. Add the potatoes and garlic. Pour in the broth and sprinkle the Italian seasoning all over the top.

2. Cook on high for 4 hours or low for 8 hours.

3. Remove pork from slow cooker and let sit 5 minutes before slicing.

DID YOU KNOW?

Not only did John Wayne star in the 1961 Western *The Comancheros*—he jumped behind the camera as well. Duke took over for director Michael Curtiz when the latter was too ill to keep filming, and later refused to be billed as co-director.

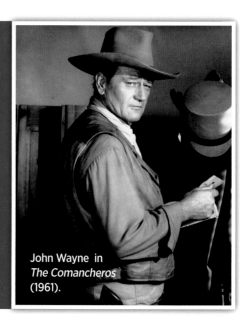

John Wayne in *The Comancheros* (1961).

Duke's SPAGHETTI ALLA CARBONARA

YEAH, YOU CAN HAVE BACON WITH YOUR PASTA IN THIS UNFORGETTABLE ITALIAN CLASSIC.

Serves 2

PROVISIONS

8 oz. spaghetti

4 slices thick-cut pepper bacon, cut into ¼-inch slices

4 large egg yolks

2 Tbsp. heavy cream

½ cup grated Parmesan cheese

DIRECTIONS

1. Bring a pot of well-salted water to a boil, add the spaghetti and cook 6 to 8 minutes or until al dente. While the water is boiling, fry the bacon pieces in a large skillet over medium-high until crispy. Do not drain off the bacon fat. Keep warm.

2. Whisk the egg yolks with the cream and half the cheese. When the pasta is done, add about 2 or 3 Tbsp. of the hot pasta water to the egg mixture and whisk. Drain the spaghetti and add it to the skillet with the bacon. Stir the spaghetti so that it absorbs the bacon flavor.

3. With the skillet off the heat, pour the egg mixture into the skillet and stir quickly. Serve immediately with the remaining Parmesan on the side.

Dean Martin and John Wayne whip up spaghetti.

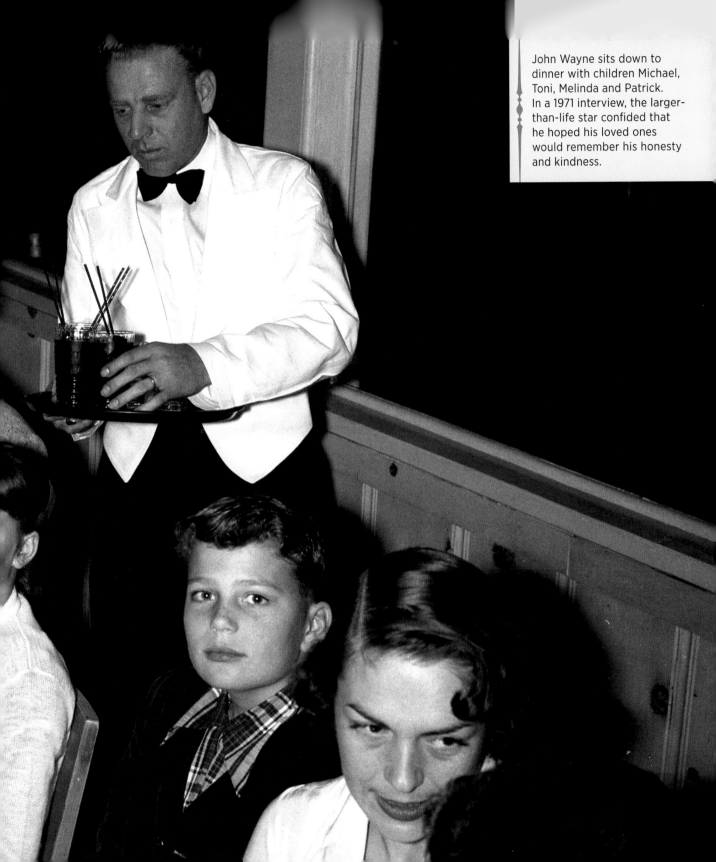

John Wayne sits down to dinner with children Michael, Toni, Melinda and Patrick. In a 1971 interview, the larger-than-life star confided that he hoped his loved ones would remember his honesty and kindness.

Golden State
SPAGHETTI WITH EGGPLANT & PEPPERS

EGGPLANT KEEPS THIS PASTA LIGHT WITHOUT SACRIFICING ANY OF ITS LIP-SMACKING GOODNESS.

Serves 4

PROVISIONS

1 medium eggplant,
peeled and cut into 1-inch cubes

2 red bell peppers, seeds and stems
removed, cut into 1-inch cubes

2 Tbsp. olive oil,
plus more for drizzling

1 tsp. kosher salt

½ tsp. freshly ground black pepper

1 whole head of garlic

1 lb. spaghetti

1 (14-oz.) can fire roasted tomatoes

DIRECTIONS

1. Preheat oven to 400 degrees F.
Put the eggplant and peppers
on a rimmed baking sheet,
drizzle with 2 Tbsp. olive oil,
and season with salt and pepper.
Toss well to coat. Cut the top off
the garlic to expose the cloves,
drizzle liberally with olive oil, and sprinkle with salt and pepper. Wrap
in foil and place on the baking sheet with the eggplant and peppers.
Roast for 40 to 45 minutes, stirring once or twice while roasting, until
the vegetables are tender and starting to brown.

2. Bring a large pot of heavily-salted water to a boil. Add the spaghetti
and cook according to the package directions. Reserve ½ cup of the
starchy cooking water and drain the pasta.

3. Heat the tomatoes in a large
skillet over medium-high.
Squeeze the garlic into the
tomatoes and stir. Add the
roasted eggplant and peppers.
Bring to a boil, then add the
starchy cooking water and boil
until the sauce slightly reduces,
about 3 to 4 minutes. Turn off
the heat, add the spaghetti, and
toss to coat. Taste and season
with more salt and pepper if
desired. Drizzle with some
olive oil and serve.

Duke in
*In Old
California*
(1942).

Stuffed
FLANK STEAK PINWHEELS
with Sautéed Spinach

**SEND HUNGER PACKING WITH THESE ALL-IN-ONE
PICTURE-PERFECT CROWD-PLEASERS.**

Serves 4

PROVISIONS

1¼ lb. flank steak

Kosher or fine sea salt, to taste

Freshly ground black pepper, to taste

1 (5.2-oz.) container Garlic and Herb Cheese, such as Boursin

⅔ cup sun-dried tomatoes in olive oil

2 (6-oz.) bags pre-washed baby spinach

⅓ cup pine nuts

3 Tbsp. olive oil plus more for preparing the meat

DIRECTIONS

1. Preheat oven to 375 degrees F. Place the flank steak between two pieces of plastic wrap. Pound with the pronged side of a meat tenderizer until it is even in thickness and about ¼-inch thick (or ask your butcher to run the steak through their meat tenderizer and then pound it with a rolling pin). Season the meat with salt and pepper. Spread half of the cheese in a 3-inch wide strip down the center of the meat.

2. Drain and finely chop the sun-dried tomatoes and place on top of the cheese. Top with about 1½ cups spinach leaves and sprinkle lightly with salt and pepper. Roll the steak up tightly, starting at one edge of the long side, tucking in the filling as you go. Using kitchen twine, tie the roast at 2-inch intervals. Brush the meat on the outside with olive oil and season well with salt and pepper.

3. Heat an oven-proof skillet over medium high. Sear the meat on all sides until browned, about 2 minutes per side. Place in the oven and cook for 25 minutes and let rest while preparing the spinach and sauce. Place the pine nuts in a large dry skillet over medium-high and toast until brown and fragrant, about 3 to 4 minutes. Remove the pine nuts and reserve. Add 1 Tbsp. olive oil to the hot pan and add the remaining spinach. Sauté until the spinach is wilted, 3 to 4 minutes. Stir the pine nuts into the spinach.

4. Place the remaining cheese in a blender or small food processor with 2 Tbsp. olive oil, 2 Tbsp. water and a large pinch of salt and pepper. Process until smooth. (If sauce is too thick, add a few more drops of water.) Slice the roast into pinwheels. Serve on the bed of spinach. drizzled with sauce.

Lone Star
SKILLET MAC AND CHEESE

LET 'EM KNOW THERE'S A NEW SHERIFF IN TOWN BY SERVING THIS ULTIMATE COMFORT FOOD FOR YOUR MAIN COURSE.

Serves 6

PROVISIONS

1 lb. short cut pasta such as elbows, spirals or bow ties

1 tsp. kosher or fine sea salt

3 cups water

1 (12-oz.) can evaporated milk

1 (10-oz.) can diced tomatoes and green chilies, undrained

2 cups grated Mexican cheese blend

Black pepper, to taste

Paprika for garnish

DIRECTIONS

1. Combine the pasta, salt and water in a large skillet. Bring to a boil over high heat. Cook, stirring occasionally, until almost all of the water is gone and the pasta is tender.

2. Add the evaporated milk and tomatoes. Bring to a boil. Reduce heat to medium and cook until the mixture thickens, about 5 minutes.

3. Add the cheese and cook, stirring, until the cheese is melted. Add additional salt and pepper to taste. Sprinkle the top with paprika and serve.

DID YOU KNOW?

John Wayne's prolific career on the silver screen spanned more than four decades. And more than 40 years after his passing, he remains a larger-than-life icon as well as one of America's most beloved actors, according to the annual Harris Poll.

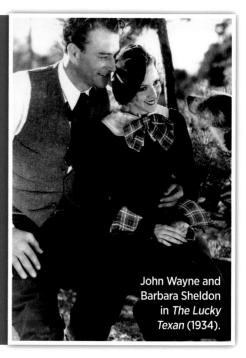

John Wayne and Barbara Sheldon in *The Lucky Texan* (1934).

Tex Mex
BEEF STEW

PUT SOME MEAT ON YOUR BONES WITH EVERY BRAWNY SPOONFUL OF THIS BORDERTOWN CLASSIC.

Serves 6

PROVISIONS

2 lb. beef stew meat, cut into 1- to 1½-inch cubes

Kosher or fine sea salt, to taste

Black pepper, to taste

1 Tbsp. olive oil

1 (15-oz.) can black beans, undrained

1 cup chunky salsa

1 cup beef broth

1 lb. baby gold potatoes, cleaned

DIRECTIONS

1. Season the beef with salt and pepper.

2. Heat the oil in a large stock pot or Dutch oven over medium high until hot. Add the beef and brown on all sides.

3. Add the beans and liquid, salsa and beef broth. Bring to a boil, cover the pan, reduce heat to simmer and cook for 2 hours. Add the potatoes and simmer for another 30 to 45 minutes or until the potatoes and beef are tender.

John Wayne and the cast of *The Alamo* (1960).

Whole ROASTED SNAPPER with Chimichurri Sauce

SCALE UP YOUR NEXT SHINDIG AND MAKE A SPLASH AT MEALTIME WITH THIS FLAVORFUL DISH.

Serves 4-6

PROVISIONS

1 (3-4 lb.) whole red snapper or grouper, gutted and scaled

Olive oil

1 lemon, sliced, plus more wedges for serving

Kosher or fine sea salt, to taste

Freshly ground black pepper, to taste

1 (8-oz.) jar chimichurri sauce

DIRECTIONS

1. Preheat oven to 450 degrees F. Line a baking sheet with parchment paper.

2. Rinse the fish, inside and out, and pat dry. Cut slits into the skin with a sharp knife, about 1 inch apart. Season the fish, inside and out, with salt and pepper. Rub the outside of the fish with olive oil. Brush some of the chimichurri sauce in the cavity of the fish. Place the lemon slices in the cavity and roast the fish for 20 to 25 minutes or until it starts to flake easily.

3. Spoon some of the chimichurri sauce over the fish and serve the rest on the side. Serve with lemon wedges, if desired.

John Wayne in *The Sea Chase* (1955).

Wayne Family Tip

Feel free to spoon the chimichurri sauce onto other tempting grilled meats, such as skirt steak, chicken and pork chops, or use it to top off grilled vegetables.

Loaded Potato
Skins, pg. 180

SNACKS

TIDE OVER ANY APPETITE WITH THESE IN-BETWEEN BITES.

Barbecue POPCORN

SERVE THIS SMOKY, SALTY SNACK ON YOUR NEXT MOVIE NIGHT —ESPECIALLY IF YOU'RE WATCHING A DUKE FLICK.

Makes about 8 cups

PROVISIONS

1 Tbsp. vegetable oil

½ cup popcorn kernels

8 Tbsp. (1 stick) butter, melted

2 Tbsp. Rocky Mountain Barbecue Seasoning (see pg. 224)

½ cup grated Parmesan cheese

Kosher or fine sea salt and pepper, to taste

DIRECTIONS

1. Heat oil in a heavy-bottomed pot with a lid over medium heat. Drop a few kernels of popcorn into the pot to test the heat—when they begin to pop, add the rest of the kernels. Cover the pan and shake while cooking until the kernels stop popping.

2. Remove from heat, add the butter, barbecue seasoning and Parmesan cheese. Stir well. Season to taste with salt and pepper.

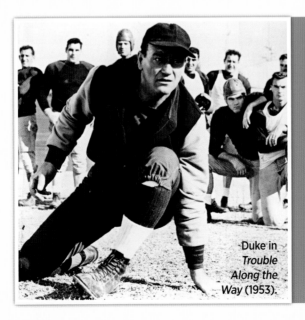

Duke in *Trouble Along the Way* (1953).

DID YOU KNOW?

Like Duke, several other men who worked on *Trouble Along the Way* once played football for USC: stuntman Tom Hennesy, Bill Radovich (in an uncredited role), assistant director Russell Saunders and technical advisor Jeff Cravath.

COWBOY BARK

AFTER JUST ONE BITE OF THIS DELICIOUSLY ADDICTIVE CHOCOLATE-COVERED SNACK, THE WHOLE FAMILY WILL BE HOOKED IN NO TIME.

Makes about 2 cups

PROVISIONS

1 cup sweetened coconut flakes

2 cups semisweet chocolate chips

1½ cups pretzel sticks, roughly chopped

8 chocolate sandwich cookies, roughly chopped

1 cup almonds, chopped

DIRECTIONS

1. Line a baking sheet with parchment paper.

2. Place the coconut in a dry skillet over medium heat and toast until golden and fragrant, about 3 minutes. Let cool.

3. Place the chocolate chips in a microwave-safe bowl and heat at high power until the chocolate is mostly melted, 1½ to 2 minutes. Stir until fully melted and glossy. Pour the chocolate onto the prepared pan and, using a spatula, spread into an even layer.

4. Immediately top the chocolate with the pretzels, cookies, almonds and toasted coconut. Refrigerate for an hour or until hardened. Break into pieces and serve.

Duke in *The Dawn Rider* (1935).

166

Wayne Family Tip

You can make this treat last even longer by storing your bark in an airtight container. Pop it into the fridge and it'll keep for up to 2 weeks. Assuming you want to wait that long.

Old West OVEN JERKY

FOR A DOWN-HOME TREAT THAT'S HARD TO BEAT, LOOK NO FURTHER THAN THIS TASTY, PROTEIN-PACKED FAVORITE.

Makes about 10 Servings

PROVISIONS

2 pounds flank steak

⅓ **cup honey**

¼ **cup soy sauce**

¼ **cup balsamic vinegar**

2 Tbsp. Worcestershire sauce

2 tsp. chipotle chili powder or regular chili powder

2 tsp. kosher or fine sea salt

1 tsp. black pepper

DIRECTIONS

1. Cut the meat into ½-inch strips. Place in a sealable food storage bag.

2. Whisk together the honey, soy sauce, vinegar, Worcestershire sauce, chili powder, salt and pepper, then pour into the bag with the meat. Refrigerate overnight or up to 3 days.

3. Position an oven rack at the top and remove any other racks from the oven. Line the bottom of the oven with foil to catch any drips.

4. Remove the meat from the marinade, pat the meat dry and discard the marinade. Stick a toothpick through the end of each strip of meat. Arrange each slice of meat between the grates of the oven rack so that the toothpick rests on the grates and the meat hangs down. Avoid letting the meat touch the oven rack and keep some space between each piece of meat.

5. Set the oven temperature to 200 degrees F and bake for 2 hours or until the meat is dry but still pliable. Carefully remove the meat from the oven, remove the toothpicks, and let the jerky dry completely. (Can be stored in an airtight container for up to 2 weeks in the refrigerator.)

John Wayne and Ben Johnson in *She Wore a Yellow Ribbon* (1949).

Donald Douglas, John Wayne and Ella Raines in *Tall in the Saddle* (1944). The first John Wayne film to be broadcast on American network television, it also featured Duke's friends Ward Bond and Gabby Hayes.

Telegraph TRAIL MIX

THIS FIVE-INGREDIENT TRAIL MIX IS THE PERFECT SNACKING COMPANION WHETHER YOU'RE HOME ON THE RANGE OR EXPLORING THE WILD FRONTIER.

Makes about 10 cups

PROVISIONS

3 cups rice or corn Chex cereal

3 cups miniature pretzels

1 (12-oz.) bag (about 2 cups) semi-sweet chocolate chips

1 (8.75-oz.) can deluxe roasted, salted nuts (about 1½ cups)

1½ cups dried mixed berries

DIRECTIONS

1. Combine all ingredients in a large mixing bowl. Store in an airtight container. (Will keep for about 5 days.)

Marceline Day, Otis Harlan and John Wayne in *The Telegraph Trail* (1933).

DID YOU KNOW?

Four years after appearing with John Wayne in *The Telegraph Trail* (1933), vaudeville actor Otis Harlan lent his voice to "Happy," one of the Seven Dwarfs in *Snow White and the Seven Dwarfs*.

Sweet & Spicy NUTS

THESE SWEET AND SPICY NUTS MAKE FOR A SNACK YOU'LL WANT TO BRING ON EVERY ADVENTURE.

Makes 4 cups

PROVISIONS

¼ cup unsalted butter

½ cup maple syrup

2 tsp. chili powder

1 tsp. kosher or fine sea salt

½ tsp. hot sauce

4 cups deluxe roasted and salted mixed nuts

DIRECTIONS

1. Preheat oven to 300 degrees F. Line a baking sheet with parchment paper.

2. In a small saucepan over medium heat, combine the butter, maple syrup, chili powder, salt and hot sauce. Bring to a boil then reduce heat and simmer for 2 minutes.

3. Place the nuts in a mixing bowl, add the maple glaze and stir well. Spread in an even layer on the prepared pan. Bake for 30 minutes, stirring every 10 minutes. Let cool, stirring occasionally to prevent sticking.

John Wayne and Lauren Bacall in *Blood Alley* (1955).

DID YOU KNOW?

Lauren Bacall's husband, Humphrey Bogart, had initially been considered to play Capt. Tom Wilder in *Blood Alley*. John Wayne joined forces with Bacall one last time for his final film, *The Shootist* (1976).

Perfect PIMENTO CHEESE

THIS SPICY SOUTHERN CHEESE DIP BRINGS THE HEAT—JUST THE WAY DUKE WOULD HAVE LIKED IT.

Serves 4

PROVISIONS

16 oz. sharp cheddar cheese, grated (4 cups grated)

8 oz. cream cheese, at room temperature

¼ cup mayonnaise

1 (7-oz.) jar pimentos, drained

1-2 tsp. hot sauce

½ tsp. kosher or fine sea salt

½ tsp. black pepper

DIRECTIONS

1. Blend the cheddar, cream cheese and mayonnaise together in a food processor or mixer until creamy and well combined. Add the pimentos, hot sauce, salt and pepper and mix well.

2. Serve with crackers or celery sticks.

DID YOU KNOW?

In *The Sons of Katie Elder* (1965), John Wayne's character, John Elder, is seen firing a Colt 1873 Single Action Army revolver. Duke bequeathed his extensive firearm collection to the National Cowboy & Western Heritage Museum in Oklahoma City, Oklahoma.

John Wayne in *The Sons of Katie Elder* (1965).

BBQ DEVILED EGGS

DRESS UP YOUR FAVORITE CLASSIC SOUTHERN STAPLE WITH A BOLD KICK OF SMOKY WESTERN FLAVOR.

Makes 24

PROVISIONS

12 hard boiled eggs, peeled

6 Tbsp. mayonnaise

2 tsp. Dijon mustard

Kosher or fine sea salt, to taste

Black pepper, to taste

4 Tbsp. barbecue sauce

2 green onions, minced

DIRECTIONS

1. Slice the eggs in half and scoop out the yolks into a small mixing bowl. Mash the yolks well with a fork. Add the mayonnaise, mustard and a pinch of salt and pepper. Mix until very smooth. Pipe or spoon the filling back into the whites.

2. Place the barbecue sauce in a squeeze bottle and drizzle some sauce over each egg. Garnish with the green onions.

Duke in *The Big Stampede* (1932).

DID YOU KNOW?

John Wayne performed all of his own stunts in *The Big Stampede*. Seeking to capitalize on Duke's newfound success and stardom following his lead role in 1939's *Stagecoach*, Warner Bros. rereleased *The Big Stampede* in 1940.

Loaded POTATO SKINS

WHEN YOU SERVE THESE LOADED POTATO SKINS AT THE NEXT BIG GAME, EVERYONE WILL FEEL LIKE A WINNER.

Serves 4-6

PROVISIONS

4 medium russet potatoes

Olive oil

Kosher or fine sea salt, to taste

Black pepper, to taste

4 slices bacon

6 oz. (1½ cups) grated sharp cheddar cheese

½ cup sour cream, plus more for serving

4 green onions, thinly sliced

DIRECTIONS

1. Preheat oven to 400 degrees F. Line a baking sheet with foil.

2. Scrub and dry the potatoes then prick all over with a fork. Rub with olive oil and sprinkle with a little salt and pepper. Place on a baking sheet and bake for 1 hour. Let cool until cool enough to handle.

3. While the potatoes bake, fry the bacon until crispy then drain on paper towels and crumble. Reserve the bacon fat.

4. Preheat the broiler and place the top rack about 6 inches from the heat source. Cut potatoes in half horizontally and scoop out the insides into a medium mixing bowl. Brush some of the reserved bacon fat on the potato skins. Place them, cut side down, back on the baking sheet and broil for 2 minutes. Leave the broiler on.

5. Add cheese and ½ cup sour cream to the potatoes and mash well. Season to taste with salt and pepper. Mound the mixture back into the skins and place back under the broiler for about 4 minutes or until the cheese has melted and is starting to brown in places. Top with the bacon, green onions and a dollop of sour cream.

Wayne Family Tip

For a lighter variation on this classic, substitute a dollop of fat-free Greek yogurt for the sour cream. You can also swap out the bacon with prosciutto, a healthier alternative that's just as tasty.

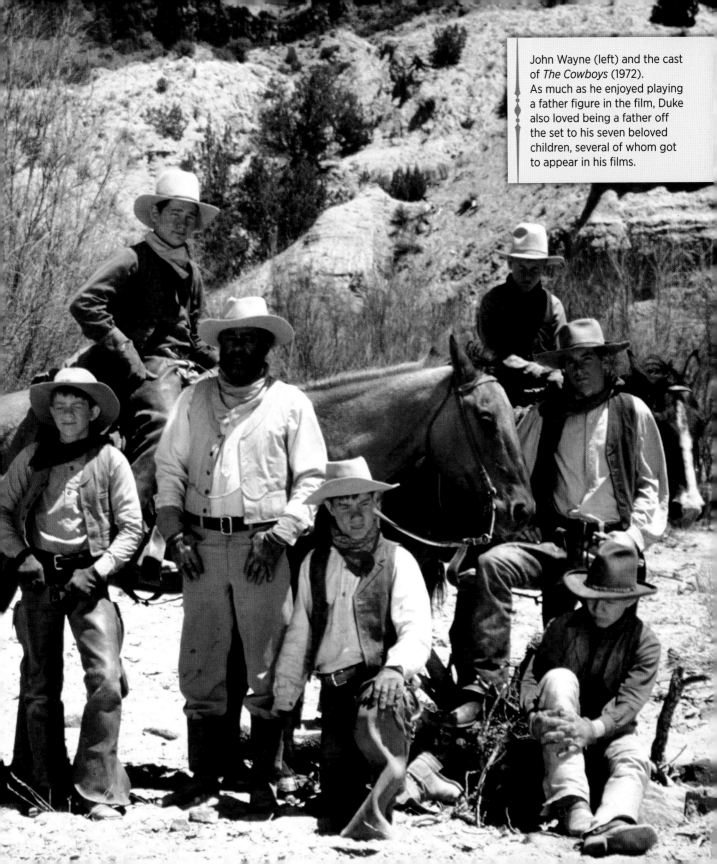

John Wayne (left) and the cast of *The Cowboys* (1972). As much as he enjoyed playing a father figure in the film, Duke also loved being a father off the set to his seven beloved children, several of whom got to appear in his films.

Gaucho FRIES

A COUPLE OF MINUTES IN THE OVEN WILL PREP THESE GOLDEN, GARLICKY FRIES FOR MAXIMUM CRUNCHY GOODNESS.

Serves 4-6

PROVISIONS

1 (32-oz.) package frozen crinkle cut French fries

2 Tbsp. olive oil

4 garlic cloves, minced

½ cup chopped fresh Italian parsley

1 tsp. kosher or fine sea salt

DIRECTIONS

1. Cook the fries per the package directions. Remove from oven but leave the oven on. Pour the fries into a large mixing bowl.

2. Heat the oil in a small skillet over medium heat. Add the garlic and cook for about 30 seconds, being careful not to burn the garlic. Pour the oil over the fries and toss well, then place the fries onto the baking sheet.

3. Place back in the oven for 2 minutes. Remove from oven, sprinkle with parsley and salt. Mix everything together well and serve immediately.

DID YOU KNOW?

John Wayne's strong physical resemblance to silent film star Ken Maynard helped him land the lead role in *The Man from Monterey* (1933), a film based on Maynard's 1928 Western *The Canyon of Adventure*.

Hondo's
NO-BAKE HONEY OAT BARS

SKIP THE OVEN AND AND POP THESE LIGHTLY SWEETENED OATS STRAIGHT INTO THE FRIDGE FOR A WHOLESOME SNACK THAT'LL FIRM UP IN JUST A FEW HOURS.

Makes 10 Bars

PROVISIONS

3 cups quick-cook oats

1 tsp. kosher or fine sea salt

1 cup almond butter

½ cup coconut oil

½ cup honey

1½ cups dried apricots, chopped

1 cup blanched slivered almonds

DIRECTIONS

1. Line a 9- by 9-inch square cake pan with parchment paper, allowing the paper to overhang the sides of the pan.

2. In a large mixing bowl, combine oats and salt. In a medium saucepan, combine almond butter, coconut oil and honey and heat over low heat until melted.

3. Pour the almond butter mixture into the oats and stir well to combine. Stir in the apricots and almonds. Press the mixture evenly and firmly into the prepared pan. Refrigerate at least 4 hours. Using the parchment paper, remove the firmed mixture from the pan and cut into 10 rectangles.

NOTE: If you don't have a 9-inch square pan, you can use a 9- by 13-inch pan, which will produce a larger batch of thinner bars.

John Wayne in *Hondo* (1953).

Buffalo TATER TOTS

IF YOU HAPPEN TO SHARE DUKE'S AFFINITY FOR ALL THINGS SPICY, THESE TATER TOTS PACK THE PERFECT AMOUNT OF HEAT.

Serves 6

PROVISIONS

1 (28-oz.) bag frozen tater tots

2 Tbsp. butter

2 Tbsp. hot sauce (such as Frank's)

3 oz. blue cheese crumbles

4 green onions, chopped

Kosher or fine sea salt, to taste

DIRECTIONS

1. Cook the tater tots according to the package directions. While they are cooking, heat the butter and hot sauce together in a small saucepan over medium heat. Pour the sauce into a large mixing bowl.

2. Once the tater tots are fully baked, add them to the butter and hot sauce mixture. Toss to coat, then top with the blue cheese crumbles and green onions. Season to taste with salt and pepper.

DID YOU KNOW?

Directed by Raoul Walsh, *The Big Trail* (1930) saw John Wayne star in his first leading role. It is one of nine Duke films selected by the Library of Congress for preservation in the National Film Registry.

Cowboy SALSA

THIS CLASSIC MIX OF PEAS, BEANS, CORN AND TOMATOES COMES TOGETHER IN A PINCH AND WILL PLEASE EVEN THE PICKIEST COWPOKES.

Serves 4-6

PROVISIONS

1 (15-oz.) can black eyed peas, drained and rinsed

1 (15-oz.) can black beans, drained and rinsed

2 cups frozen corn kernels, thawed

1 can tomatoes and chilies (such as Ro*Tel®), drained

½ cup chopped fresh cilantro

¼ cup olive oil

2 Tbsp. red wine vinegar

1 tsp. kosher or fine sea salt

½ tsp. pepper

DIRECTIONS

1. Combine all ingredients in a medium mixing bowl. Cover and refrigerate until serving.

John Wayne and Sean Kelly saddle up in *The Cowboys* (1972).

DID YOU KNOW?

Based on the novel by William Dale Jennings, *The Cowboys* spawned a 1974 television series of the same name that explored the boys' ranching adventures following Wil Andersen's death in the film.

Cherry Dump Cake,
pg. 200

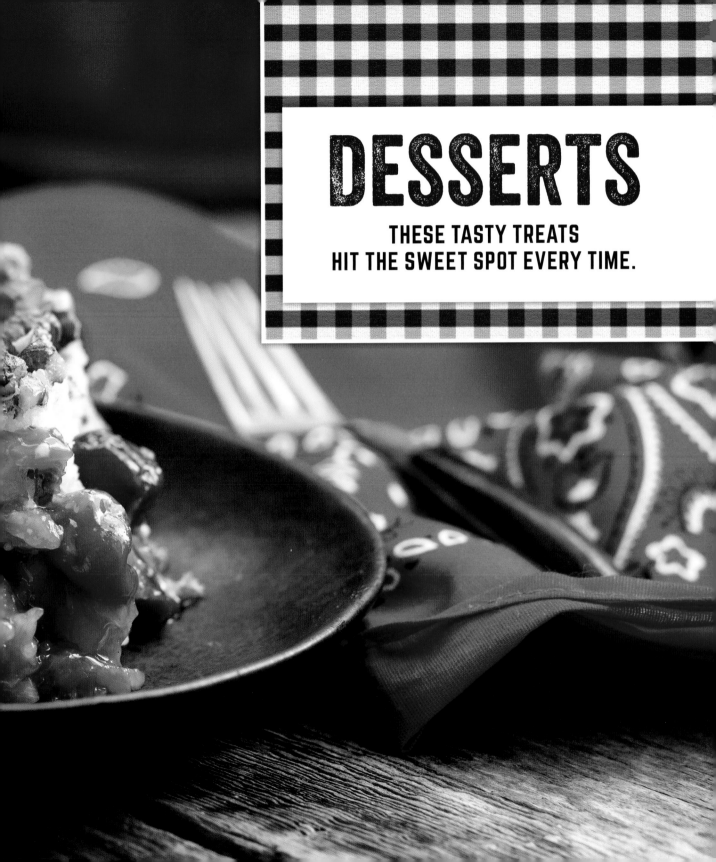

DESSERTS

THESE TASTY TREATS
HIT THE SWEET SPOT EVERY TIME.

Pioneer BUTTERMILK PUDDING with Caramel Sauce

A FEW SCOOPS OF THIS BUTTERY DESSERT WILL KEEP YOUR KIN SMILING UNTIL THE COWS COME HOME.

Serves 4

PROVISIONS

1 (¼-oz.) packet unflavored gelatin

1½ cups half-and-half, divided

1¼ cups sugar, divided

¾ tsp. kosher or fine sea salt, divided

2 cups buttermilk

3 tsp. pure vanilla extract, divided

FOR THE PUDDING

1. Sprinkle the gelatin over 2 Tbsp. of water and let set for 5 minutes.

2. In a medium saucepan over medium-low heat, combine 1 cup half-and-half, ¾ cup sugar and ¼ tsp. salt. Simmer for 5 minutes, stirring to dissolve the sugar. Reduce the heat to low and add the gelatin and buttermilk. Remove from the heat and add 2 tsp. vanilla.

3. Pour the mixture into four (8-oz.) ramekins and let cool to room temperature. Refrigerate for at least 3 hours or up to 2 days.

FOR THE CARAMEL SAUCE

1. Put the remaining ½ cup sugar in a deep saucepan. Add 2 Tbsp. water and cook over medium heat until the sugar dissolves. Continue to cook, swirling the pan as needed (do not stir) until the mixture becomes the color of an old penny, for about 10 minutes.

2. Take the saucepan off the heat and add ½ cup half-and-half. The mixture will bubble up furiously. Once it stops bubbling, add 1 tsp. vanilla and ½ tsp. salt. Stir until the sauce is smooth. Let cool then refrigerate, covered, until ready to use. (Can be made up to 2 weeks ahead.)

3. To serve, dip the ramekins briefly into hot water, place a serving plate on top and invert. Drizzle the puddings with the caramel sauce and serve.

Quick-Draw MEXICAN CHOCOLATE MOUSSE

WARM, SWEET CINNAMON KICKS THIS CLASSIC CROWD-PLEASER UP A NOTCH, FROM EXCELLENT TO IRRESISTIBLE.

Serves 2

PROVISIONS

1 ¼ cups heavy whipping cream, divided

¼ cup unsweetened cocoa powder, sifted, plus more for dusting

¼ cup powdered sugar

1 tsp. pure vanilla extract

½ tsp. ground cinnamon

DIRECTIONS

1. Whip the cream until soft peaks form and remove 2 Tbsp. for garnish.

2. Add the remaining ingredients and whip until stiff (but not dry) peaks form. Do not over beat!

3. Dollop half the reserved cream on top of each mousse and dust with a little cocoa powder before serving.

DID YOU KNOW?

George Sherman directed John Wayne in eight "Three Mesquiteers" films beginning with *Pals of the Saddle* in 1938 and ending with *New Frontier* (1939). The two teamed up one last time to make Sherman's final film, the 1971 classic *Big Jake*.

John Wayne in *Pals of the Saddle* (1938).

Blue Ribbon BERRY FOOL

SERVE UP HEAPING HELPINGS OF THIS BERRIES-AND-CREAM DELIGHT AND THE ONLY BOLD TALK YOU'LL GET IS ENDLESS PRAISE.

Serves 4

PROVISIONS

12 oz. fresh raspberries
(or any berries)

1 Tbsp. sugar

1 cup heavy whipping cream

2 Tbsp. organic powdered sugar

1 Tbsp. coarsely chopped
pistachios (optional garnish)

DIRECTIONS

1. Put half the raspberries in a bowl with 1 Tbsp. sugar and mash with a fork.

2. Whip the cream with the powdered sugar until stiff peaks form. Do not over-whip the cream.

3. With a slotted spoon, spoon the mashed raspberries into the whipped cream (discard the raspberry juices) and lightly fold the raspberries into the cream, leaving it streaky.

4. Spoon half of the whipped cream/raspberry mixture into 4 small dessert bowls and top with half the whole raspberries, the remaining cream and the remaining raspberries. Garnish with chopped pistachios if desired.

Duke at the L.A. Country Sheriff's Rodeo in 1949.

Quick-Draw
MEXICAN CHOCOLATE MOUSSE

WARM, SWEET CINNAMON KICKS THIS CLASSIC CROWD-PLEASER UP A NOTCH, FROM EXCELLENT TO IRRESISTIBLE.

Serves 2

PROVISIONS

1 ¼ cups heavy whipping cream, divided

¼ cup unsweetened cocoa powder, sifted, plus more for dusting

¼ cup powdered sugar

1 tsp. pure vanilla extract

½ tsp. ground cinnamon

DIRECTIONS

1. Whip the cream until soft peaks form and remove 2 Tbsp. for garnish.

2. Add the remaining ingredients and whip until stiff (but not dry) peaks form. Do not over beat!

3. Dollop half the reserved cream on top of each mousse and dust with a little cocoa powder before serving.

DID YOU KNOW?

George Sherman directed John Wayne in eight "Three Mesquiteers" films beginning with *Pals of the Saddle* in 1938 and ending with *New Frontier* (1939). The two teamed up one last time to make Sherman's final film, the 1971 classic *Big Jake.*

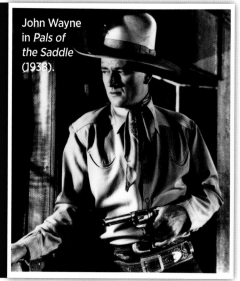

John Wayne in *Pals of the Saddle* (1938).

CHERRY DUMP CAKE

TAKE A SEAT, PILGRIM, AND THROW THESE CHERRY FIXINGS STRAIGHT IN THE OVEN FOR A MOUTHWATERING DESSERT THAT PRACTICALLY MAKES ITSELF.

Serves 8

PROVISIONS

Oil for preparing the dish

1 (21-oz.) can cherry pie filling

1 (20-oz.) can crushed pineapple in juice, undrained

1 box yellow cake mix

12 Tbsp. cold butter, cut into small pieces

¾ cup chopped pecans

DIRECTIONS

1. Preheat oven to 350 degrees F. Oil a 9- by 13-inch baking dish.

2. Pour the cherry pie filling and pineapple, along with the juices, in the prepared baking dish, then stir to combine. Sprinkle the cake mix evenly over the top.

3. Dot the butter all over the top of the cake mix, then sprinkle with pecans. Bake for 50 to 60 minutes or until the topping is golden brown.

John Wayne and Vera Ralston in *Dakota* (1945).

DID YOU KNOW?

Before moving to Hollywood, Duke's Czech-born *Dakota* costar Vera Ralston competed in figure skating at the 1936 Olympics, where she reportedly made a point of insulting Adolf Hitler to his face.

The Best Darn CHOCOLATE CHIP COOKIES

FILL YOUR HOME WITH THE AROMA OF HAPPY CHILDHOOD MEMORIES (OR MAKE SOME NEW ONES WITH YOUR YOUNG'UNS) WITH THIS FOOLPROOF FAVORITE.

Makes about 24 cookies, depending on the size

PROVISIONS

1 cup creamy almond butter

1 cup semisweet chocolate chips

1 cup brown sugar

2 large eggs

1 Tbsp. pure vanilla extract

DIRECTIONS

1. Preheat oven to 350 degrees F. Line 2 baking sheets with parchment paper or silicone baking mats.

2. Combine all the ingredients in a large mixing bowl and stir well. Drop 1 Tbsp. of batter onto the prepared baking sheets and flatten gently with a spatula.

3. Bake for 10 to 12 minutes. Let cool.

John Wayne and Nancy Olson in *Big Jim McLain* (1952).

DID YOU KNOW?

Before co-starring with John Wayne in *Big Jim McLain* (1952), Nancy Olson received an Academy Award nomination for her portrayal of Betty Schaefer in the 1950 film noir *Sunset Boulevard.*

Rich and Tasty
CHOCOLATE POTS

TURN ANY MEAL INTO A LAVISH AFFAIR BY DISHING OUT TOOTHSOME CUPS OF SILKY CHOCOLATE BLISS.

Serves 6

PROVISIONS

1 (13.5-oz.) can coconut milk (full fat, not light)

9 oz. (about 1 ½ cups) chocolate chips

1 tsp. pure vanilla extract

1 large egg, lightly beaten

Berries for garnish (optional)

DIRECTIONS

1. Bring 2 inches of water to a simmer in a large saucepan. Turn the heat to low and keep the water at a bare simmer.

2. Shake the can of coconut milk well, then pour into a heatproof mixing bowl. Set the bowl over the pan of simmering water, making sure the bottom of the bowl does not touch the water. Add the chocolate and melt, stirring occasionally. Once the chocolate has melted, whisk in the vanilla and then the egg. Continue whisking until the mixture is smooth.

3. Transfer the mixture to a pitcher or spouted measuring cup and divide the mixture among 6 small tea or cappuccino cups or ramekins. Chill for 3 hours.

4. Garnish with fresh berries if desired and serve.

John Wayne and Marlene Dietrich in *Pittsburgh* (1942).

Cookies & Cream
NO-BAKE PIE

GET YOUR CHOCOLATE FIX WITHOUT THE HASSLE OF FIRING UP THE OVEN.

Serves 8

PROVISIONS

Oil for preparing the pie pan

21 chocolate sandwich cookies, divided

1 cup heavy cream

8 oz. cream cheese, softened

½ cup sugar

1 tsp. pure vanilla extract

DIRECTIONS

1. Grease a 9-inch pie pan with oil.

2. Place 12 cookies in a plastic freezer bag and pound them with a rolling pin until they turn into fine crumbs, then press the crumbs evenly and firmly into the prepared pie pan. Place the remaining cookies in the bag and break them up so there are bigger cookie pieces as well as smaller crumbs. Save a handful of crumbs to garnish the pie.

3. Using a hand-held mixer, whip the cream on high speed until stiff peaks form. Place the cream cheese, sugar and vanilla in a large mixing bowl and blend on high speed until smooth. Fold in the whipped cream and the crushed cookie pieces, then spoon the mixture into the pie pan. Garnish with the reserved crumbs and refrigerate until serving.

DID YOU KNOW?

When he wasn't hustling around a film set, fishing on the *Wild Goose* or lounging in a hammock, Duke enjoyed playing chess, poker and bridge during his down time.

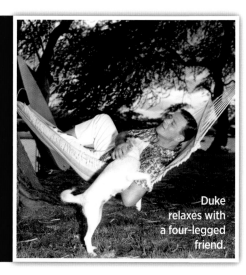

Duke relaxes with a four-legged friend.

Kenneth Tobey and John Wayne in *The Wings of Eagles* (1957). The film is based on the real-life story of Frank "Spig" Wead, a U.S. Navy aviator who learned to walk again and returned to active duty following a spinal injury.

Wayne Family Tip

For a traditional Eton Mess, substitute the blackberries for strawberries. Rhubarb or raspberries will work nicely as well. This refreshing British dessert is best enjoyed the day it's made.

Brannigan's ETON MESS

SHOW YOUR BRITISH PALS A THING OR TWO BY WHIPPING UP A BATCH OF THIS REFRESHING CLASSIC FROM ACROSS THE POND.

Serves 6

PROVISIONS

- 2 cups heavy cream
- 2 Tbsp. powdered sugar
- 10 oz. lemon curd
- 1 box vanilla meringues
- 2 pints blackberries (or any berries you like)

DIRECTIONS

1. Whip the cream with the powdered sugar. Place the lemon curd in a mixing bowl and whisk it to lighten it up. Add ¼ of the whipped cream to the lemon curd and whisk. Fold in the remaining cream.

2. Crumble the meringues roughly so that you have both larger pieces for texture plus finer pieces.

3. To assemble, start with a layer of the lemon whipped cream, top with crumbled meringues, then add berries. Repeat the layers. (Can be eaten immediately or chill for a few hours until ready to serve.)

John Wayne in *Brannigan* (1975).

Sam McCord's
FROZEN S'MORES

SATISFY YOUR SWEET TOOTH AND BEAT THE HEAT WITH THIS CHILLED TAKE ON A CLASSIC CAMPFIRE TREAT.

Serves 6

PROVISIONS

Vegetable oil, for preparing the pan

1½ pints gluten-free rocky road or chocolate ice cream

1¼ cups graham cracker crumbs

2 Tbsp. unsalted butter, melted

8 tsp. mini semisweet chocolate chips

½ cup heavy cream

DIRECTIONS

1. Oil a 6-cup (½ cup each) silicone muffin pan with oil. (Note: This recipe works best with a silicone baking pan as it makes it easier to remove the s'mores. But if all you have is a metal muffin tin, just line it with paper cupcake liners.)

2. Let the ice cream soften at room temperature for about 10 minutes (it should be easy to scoop) or microwave on high power for 30 seconds.

3. Combine the graham cracker crumbs and melted butter until fully mixed. Place 1 heaping Tbsp. into each of the 6 cups of the muffin pan and press down firmly. Reserve the remaining crumbs for garnish. Sprinkle 1 tsp. of chocolate chips into the bottom of each cup on top of the crust and reserve the remaining chips for garnish. Scoop ½ cup of ice cream into each cup, then press down firmly with the bottom of a glass. Freeze until firm for 1 to 2 hours.

4. Whip the cream until stiff peaks form. Remove the s'mores from the muffin pan by pushing on the bottom of each muffin cup and popping them out. Top with the whipped cream and garnish with the remaining crumbs and chocolate chips.

Capucine and John Wayne in *North to Alaska* (1960).

Tropical KEY LIME PIE

ONE BITE OF THIS DELIGHTFUL DESSERT WILL HAVE YOU DREAMING OF SUNNY BEACHES AND WARM SUMMER NIGHTS.

Serves 8

PROVISIONS

1 (8-oz.) package cream cheese, at room temperature

1 (14-oz.) can sweetened condensed milk

3 egg yolks

½ cup fresh key lime or lime juice

1 pre-made graham cracker crust

DIRECTIONS

1. Preheat oven to 350 degrees F.

2. In the bowl of an electric mixer, preferably fitted with a paddle attachment, beat the cream cheese until smooth and creamy. Add the sweetened condensed milk and egg yolks and mix until fully incorporated, scraping down the sides of the bowl as needed. Add the lime juice and beat well.

3. Pour the mixture into the pie shell and smooth the top with a spatula. Place the pie on a baking sheet and cook for 10 minutes or until filling begins to set. Let cool completely. Refrigerate for at least 2 hours or up to 24 hours before serving.

John Wayne in a scene from *Reap the Wild Wind* (1942).

Old-Fashioned
MUDSLIDE PIE

WHEN YOU'RE HANKERING FOR CHOCOLATE AND COFFEE, THIS RECIPE HITS THE SPOT AND COMES WITH A BUZZ THAT'S OUT OF THIS WORLD.

Serves 4

PROVISIONS

22 chocolate sandwich cookies, divided

¼ cup butter, melted

6 cups coffee ice cream, softened

½ cup heavy whipping cream, whipped

¼ cup caramel syrup

DIRECTIONS

1. Place 19 cookies into a food processor fitted with the steel blade. Process until ground into fine crumbs. Add the melted butter and pulse several times to combine. Dump the mixture into a 9-inch deep dish pie pan, then press firmly and evenly on the bottom and up the sides of the pan. Freeze for 15 minutes.

2. Spread the softened ice cream into the frozen pie crust and smooth the top. Freeze for at least 4 hours or up to 2 days.

3. Coarsely crush the remaining 3 cookies. Spread the whipped cream over the ice cream layer, sprinkle the crushed cookies on top and drizzle with caramel syrup. Serve immediately or store in the freezer until ready to eat.

Maureen O'Hara and John Wayne in *McLintock!* (1963).

No-Churn
HONEY BERRY ICE CREAM

AFTER A HARD DAY'S WORK, THIS NO-FUSS DESSERT PUTS THE "SWEET" IN HOME SWEET HOME.

Serves 6-8

PROVISIONS

1 (12-oz.) bag frozen mixed berries (no need to thaw)

2 cups heavy cream

½ tsp. kosher or fine sea salt

1 (14-oz.) can sweetened condensed milk

¼ cup honey

Berries and mint for garnish (optional)

DIRECTIONS

1. Place the berries in a food processor and process until finely chopped.

2. Pour the cream and salt into the bowl of an electric mixer fitted with the whisk attachment and whip until stiff peaks form, about 2 minutes.

3. Using a spatula, fold in the berries, sweetened condensed milk and honey until fully combined. Transfer the mixture into a freezer-safe container (a 9-inch loaf pan works well) and cover, then place in the freezer until solid, about 6 hours.

4. Serve garnished with berries and mint if desired.

Duke enjoys a moment on the open water.

DID YOU KNOW?

Although he was born in Iowa, John Wayne moved with his family to California at the age of 6 and became a lifelong resident of The Golden State. He developed a particular affinity for Newport Beach.

Skillet S'MORES DIP

YOUR HUNT TO TURN A FIRESIDE FAVORITE INTO SCOOPABLE HEAVEN ENDS HERE.

Serves 6-8

PROVISIONS

1 Tbsp. butter

1 (12-oz.) bag semisweet chocolate chips

25 large marshmallows, cut in half widthwise

Graham crackers

DIRECTIONS

1. Place a 9-inch oven-proof skillet in the oven and preheat the oven to 450 degrees F. When the oven is ready, carefully remove the hot pan from the oven, add the butter and swirl to coat the pan. Add the chocolate chips in an even layer, then place the marshmallows in concentric circles over the chocolate.

2. Place back in the oven for 7 to 9 minutes or until the marshmallows are puffed and golden brown.

3. Serve hot with graham crackers for dipping.

DID YOU KNOW?

For his contributions to the Western movie genre, in 1974, Duke was inducted into the Hall of Great Western Performers in the National Cowboy and Western Heritage Museum.

John Wayne in *Blue Steel* (1934).

Wayne Family Tip

Coating your skillet evenly with butter will help ensure you don't wind up with burnt chocolate. After your skillet's been baking for 7 minutes, give it a peek to be sure the top is browning just the way you like.

Perfect Pico de
Gallo, pg. 240

SALSAS, SAUCES & MORE

ROUND OUT ANY DISH WITH THESE SATISFYING EXTRAS.

Rocky Mountain
BARBECUE SEASONING

BRING A TASTE OF THE WILD FRONTIER TO ANY DISH WITH A PINCH OF THIS TRUSTY SEASONING.

Makes about 1 cup

PROVISIONS

¼ cup brown sugar, packed

¼ cup smoked paprika

2 Tbsp. garlic powder

2 Tbsp. onion powder

1-2 Tbsp. ancho chili powder

1 Tbsp. kosher or fine sea salt

2 tsp. black pepper

DIRECTIONS

1. Combine all ingredients in a small bowl, whisking well to break up all lumps. Pour into a glass container and secure with an airtight lid. Will keep for up to one year.

John Wayne and Sheila Bromley in *Westward Ho* (1935).

225

Chipotle
LIME DRESSING

FOR A LIGHT AND TASTY SOUTHWEST FIXING YOU CAN PAIR WITH JUST ABOUT ANYTHING, THIS DRESSING'S THE GENUINE ARTICLE.

Makes about ¾ cup

PROVISIONS

- ½ cup olive oil
- ¼ cup fresh lime juice (from 2-3 limes)
- ¼ cup chopped fresh cilantro leaves
- 4 tsp. pureed chipotle in adobo sauce*
- 2 tsp. honey
- 1 tsp. ground cumin
- ¾ tsp. kosher or fine sea salt
- ¼ tsp. black pepper

DIRECTIONS

1. Combine all ingredients in a mason jar and shake well. (Can be stored in the refrigerator for 1 week, covered.)

*Create pureed chipotle in adobo sauce by blending a jar of chipotle in adobo sauce in a blender until smooth. Store in a covered jar in the refrigerator for up to 6 months. (Can be stirred into soups, stews, taco meat, chili, etc.)

Rock Hudson and John Wayne in *The Undefeated* (1969).

DID YOU KNOW?

The Undefeated (1969) was written by Stanley H. Lough, who also wrote 1968's *Bandolero* starring Duke's friends and occasional co-stars James Stewart and Dean Martin.

Buttermilk Chive RANCH DRESSING

A HALLMARK OF SOUTHERN HOSPITALITY, BUTTERMILK LENDS A TASTE OF COUNTRY LIVING TO THIS DELICIOUS HOMESTYLE DRESSING.

Makes about 2 cups

PROVISIONS

- 1 cup mayonnaise
- ¾ cup buttermilk
- 1½ tsp. garlic powder
- 1½ tsp. onion powder
- 1 tsp. kosher or fine sea salt
- ½ tsp. black pepper
- ¼ cup minced fresh chives

DIRECTIONS

1. Combine all ingredients in a mixing bowl, whisking well. Cover and refrigerate until you're ready to serve. (Can be made 3-4 days ahead.)

Louis Johnson, Ken Reafsnyder and John Wayne at the 26 Bar Ranch.

Cilantro Lime RICE

WHETHER YOU SERVE IT WITH FISH TACOS, GRILLED CHICKEN OR STEAK, THIS ENDLESSLY VERSATILE SIDE GETS THE JOB DONE RIGHT.

Serves 4

PROVISIONS

2 limes

2 cups water

1 Tbsp. vegetable or olive oil

1 tsp. kosher or fine sea salt

1 cup long grain white or basmati rice

½ cup loosely packed cilantro leaves, finely chopped

DIRECTIONS

1. Finely grate the zest of one lime and squeeze the juice from both limes.

2. Bring the water, oil, salt and lime zest to boil in a medium pot with a lid. Add the rice and cook according to the package directions.

3. Let the rice sit, covered, for 5 minutes once cooked. Add the lime juice and cilantro and mix well with a fork.

DID YOU KNOW?

Dedicated to telling the story of the Alamo correctly, Duke insisted on directing the film himself and put his own money into the production. The epic Western was released in 1960.

Duke in *The Alamo* (1960).

Five-Minute FLATBREADS

YOU CAN COUNT THE MINUTES YOU NEED TO BAKE THIS SIMPLE AND TASTY STARTER ON ONE HAND.

Serves 2

PROVISIONS

- ¾ cup flour, plus more for dusting
- 1 tsp. baking powder
- ½ tsp. kosher or fine sea salt
- 5 Tbsp. yogurt
- 1 Tbsp. honey
- 1 Tbsp. olive oil

DIRECTIONS

1. Heat a non-stick skillet over medium-high until hot. While the skillet is heating, prepare the flatbread dough.

2. In a medium mixing bowl, whisk together the flour, baking powder and salt. Add the yogurt, honey and the olive oil, then mix until it forms into a dough. Divide the dough into two equal portions.

3. Lightly flour a surface and roll the dough into an oval about 8- by 5-inches and slightly less than ¼-inch thick. Cook for about 2 minutes per side or until golden brown on both sides. Serve as is or topped with your favorite fixings.

John Wayne in *Cast a Giant Shadow* (1966).

DID YOU KNOW?

Duke's *Cast a Giant Shadow* (1966) marks Michael Douglas's movie debut as a Jeep driver.

Desperado HOT SAUCE

IT'S HIGH TIME YOU LET THE NAYSAYERS KNOW YOU WERE BORN GAME FOR LIQUID HEAT. THIS SAUCE TAKES NO PRISONERS.

Makes about 1 pint

PROVISIONS

20 red Anaheim chilies

2 jalapeño peppers

4 cloves garlic, peeled

1½ cups white wine or apple cider vinegar

½ tsp. kosher or fine sea salt

2 Tbsp. organic honey

DIRECTIONS

1. Wash the peppers and cut off the tops. Cut the chilies and peppers in half. Place in a medium saucepan along with the garlic, vinegar and salt, then bring to a boil. Cover the pan, reduce the heat and let boil very gently for 20 minutes or until the peppers and garlic cloves are very soft.

2. Pour the mixture into a blender. Remove the small plastic cap from the lid and cover with several layers of kitchen toweling. Start the blender on low and gradually increase to high. Continue to blend on high until all the seeds are pulverized and the sauce is thickened, about 2 minutes. Add the honey and blend well. Store covered in the refrigerator.

John Wayne and Dorothy Gulliver in *The Shadow of the Eagle* (1932).

Wayne Family Tip

When handling hot peppers, be careful not to touch your eyes. Bottled sauce will keep up to four months in the fridge.

Cantina Lime
SOUR CREAM

PAIR A FEW SPOONFULS OF THIS SOUR CREAM WITH ANY FLAMING HOT LATIN FARE AND THEY'LL NEVER SEE YOU SWEAT.

Makes about 1 cup

PROVISIONS

1 lime

1 cup sour cream

2 green onions, green and white parts thinly sliced

DIRECTIONS

1. Finely grate the zest of the lime and squeeze the juice, then mix both into the sour cream. Stir in the green onions and serve. (Can be made 1 day ahead. Store covered in the refrigerator.)

Martha Scott and John Wayne in *In Old Oklahoma* (1943).

Sonora
MANGO SALSA

A VIBRANT ADDITION TO ANY TABLE, THIS SWEET AND SPICY SALSA IS LOADED WITH JUICY MANGO AND LOOKS LIKE A MEXICAN SUNRISE IN A BOWL.

Serves 8

PROVISIONS

1 (16-oz.) package frozen mango chunks, thawed or 4 cups fresh mango chunks (from 3 mangos)

Juice of 2 limes

1 small red onion, diced

1 cup loosely packed cilantro leaves, chopped

2 tsp. pureed chipotle in adobo sauce (see pg. 226)

DIRECTIONS

1. Combine all ingredients in a mixing bowl, stirring well. Serve immediately or store, covered, in the refrigerator for up to 2 days.

John Wayne and Paul Fix in *Somewhere in Sonora* (1933).

DID YOU KNOW?

Between 1931 and 1973, Paul Fix and John Wayne worked on more than 25 films together. Fix also co-wrote the screenplay for Duke's 1944 flick *Tall in the Saddle* and appeared in the second pilot episode of *Star Trek*.

Perfect
PICO DE GALLO

ADD THE FINISHING TOUCH TO YOUR SOUTH-OF-THE-BORDER FEAST WITH A BOWL OF THIS AUTHENTIC, REFRESHING FAVORITE.

Serves 4-6

PROVISIONS

12 Roma tomatoes, seeded and chopped

1 large white onion, finely diced

3-4 jalapeño peppers, seeds and veins removed, finely minced

2 cups fresh cilantro, stems removed, chopped

Juice of 2 limes

Kosher salt and freshly ground black pepper, to taste

DIRECTIONS

1. Combine the tomatoes, onion, jalapeño peppers and cilantro in a large mixing bowl and stir to combine. Add the lime juice and stir to combine. Add salt and pepper to taste.

John Wayne and Kim Darby in *True Grit* (1969).

DID YOU KNOW?

Four years after the two made *The Sons of Katie Elder* (1965), *True Grit* marked John Wayne's final collaboration with director Harry Hathaway.

Red Hot CHILI SAUCE

LIKE A DESERT BLAZE IN A BOTTLE, A DASH OF THIS HOT SAUCE WILL IGNITE YOUR TASTE BUDS WITH FIERY FLAVOR.

Makes 2 cups

PROVISIONS

3 dried ancho chili peppers

2 cloves garlic, peeled and smashed

1 Tbsp. olive oil

1 tsp. kosher or fine sea salt

½ tsp. black pepper

¼ tsp. ground cloves

DIRECTIONS

1. Remove the stems and seeds from the chilies. (Be careful not to touch your eyes when working with chilies.) Place the chilies in a small saucepan and cover with water. Bring to a boil, remove from heat and let sit for 10 minutes.

2. Remove the chilies from the soaking water, reserving the water. Place the chilies, garlic, olive oil, salt, pepper and cloves in a blender. Add 1½ cups of the soaking water and blend for two minutes until the sauce is completely smooth. (Can be used immediately or stored in a covered glass container in the refrigerator for up to one week. Reheat before using.)

John Wayne and Jim Hutton in *Hellfighters* (1968).

DID YOU KNOW?

Before appearing in *Hellfighters* (1968), Jim Hutton co-starred with Duke as Sgt. Petersen in *The Green Berets* (1968).

Wayne Family Tip

This recipe also works well with pinto beans. Refried beans will keep in an airtight container in the fridge for up to four days and will last several months when frozen.

Refried BLACK BEANS

THERE'S ONLY ONE TRICK TO MAKING THIS SURE-FIRE SIDE: DOUBLING THE SERVING SIZE FROM THE GET-GO.

Serves 6

PROVISIONS

2 Tbsp. extra-virgin olive oil

2 tsp. chili powder

1 tsp. ground cumin

½ large white or yellow onion, diced

2 (15-oz.) cans black beans, drained and rinsed

¾ cup water (plus more if needed)

Kosher salt and freshly ground black pepper, to taste

3 oz. queso fresco or Monterey jack cheese, crumbled

DIRECTIONS

1. Heat the oil in a large skillet over medium high. Add the chili powder, cumin and onion. Cook until the onion is tender, about 5 minutes.

2. Add the beans plus water. Smash the beans with the back of a spoon or a potato masher and cook until the beans are heated through. If they are too thick, add a little more water. If too thin, cook a little longer. Season to taste with salt and pepper. Serve topped with the crumbled cheese.

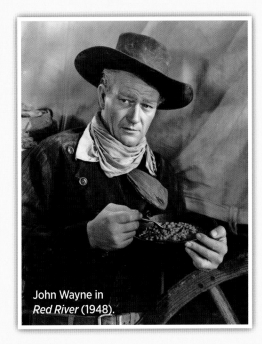

John Wayne in *Red River* (1948).

SALSA VERDE

WHEN DINNERTIME REQUIRES REINFORCEMENTS, THIS BORDERLAND STANDARD GETS THE JOB DONE RIGHT EVERY TIME.

Makes 2 cups

PROVISIONS

1½ pounds tomatillos

1 medium white onion, peeled and cut into 6 wedges

2 jalapeño peppers, cut in half, seeds and veins removed (leave seeds in for spicier sauce)

1 Tbsp. olive oil

1 tsp. kosher or fine sea salt

½ tsp. black pepper

Juice of 1 lime (2 Tbsp.)

½ cup fresh cilantro leaves

DIRECTIONS

1. Preheat oven to 400 degrees F and line a baking sheet with foil.

2. Remove the husks from the tomatillos, rinse, and cut in half. Place the tomatillos, onion and jalapeños on the prepared baking sheet. Drizzle with the oil and sprinkle with the salt and pepper. Toss to coat. Roast for 20 minutes or until the vegetables are soft.

3. Transfer the vegetables along with any juices into a blender. Add the lime juice and cilantro, then pulse several times until you have a thick, slightly chunky sauce. (Can be used immediately or stored in a covered glass container for up to one week. Serve this salsa hot or cold.)

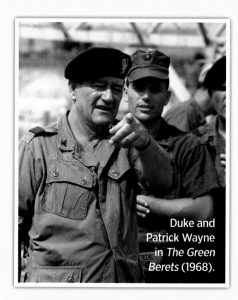

Duke and Patrick Wayne in *The Green Berets* (1968).

John Wayne spends quality time with daughter Aissa on the set of *The Alamo* (1960). Aissa later lovingly wrote of the good times she shared with her famous father in her 1991 memoir, *John Wayne: My Father*.

CONVERSION CHART

USE THIS HANDY CHART TO CONVERT CUPS AND OUNCES TO LITERS AND GRAMS.

Volume

¼ teaspoon	=	1.25 mL
½ teaspoon	=	2.50 mL
1 teaspoon	=	5 mL
1 tablespoon	=	15 mL
¼ cup	=	60 mL
⅓ cup	=	80 mL
½ cup	=	120 mL
⅔ cup	=	160 mL
¾ cup	=	180 mL
1 cup	=	240 mL
1 quart	=	1 liter
1½ quarts	=	1.5 liters
2 quarts	=	2 liters
2½ quarts	=	2.5 liters
3 quarts	=	3 liters
4 quarts	=	4 liters

Weight

1 ounce	=	30 grams
2 ounces	=	55 grams
3 ounces	=	85 grams
4 ounces (¼ pound)	=	115 grams
8 ounces (½ pound)	=	225 grams
16 ounces (1 pound)	=	455 grams
2 pounds	=	910 grams

Length

⅛ inch	=	3 mm
¼ inch	=	6 mm
½ inch	=	13 mm
¾ inch	=	19 mm
1 inch	=	2.5 cm
2 inches	=	5 cm

Temperatures

Fahrenheit		Celsius
32°	=	0°
212°	=	100°
250°	=	120°
275°	=	140°
300°	=	150°
325°	=	160°
350°	=	180°
375°	=	190°
400°	=	200°
425°	=	220°
450°	=	230°
475°	=	250°
500°	=	260°

⋙ INDEX ⋘

A

Almond(s), 166, 186
   butter, 186, 202
Apple(s), 131, 136
   cider, 131
Apricots, dried, 186
Artichoke hearts, 65
Arugula, baby, 70
Avocados, 86

B

Bacon, 17, 24, 27, 42, 45, 46, 49, 59,
   66, 69, 70, 75, 132, 149, 180
   Canadian, 28, 31
Baking powder, 13, 233
Beans
   cannellini, 99
   black, 35, 41, 80, 159, 190, 245
   black eyed peas, 190
   refried, 18
   white, 60

Beef
   brisket, 113
   chuck roast, 145
   corned, 76
   flank steak, 142, 155, 169
   ground, 90
   stew meat, 159
Berries, 172, 197, 205, 211, 219
Blackberries, 211
Bread, 90
   baguette, 55
   English muffins, 28
   multigrain, 99
Broth, *see Stock*
Brown sugar, 202, 225
Buttermilk, 117, 194, 229

C

Caramel syrup, 216
Carrots, 136
Cereal, corn Chex, 172

Cheese
   American, 28
   blue, 79, 189
   cheddar, 24, 36, 46, 69, 89, 132,
      176, 180
   cotija, 23
   cream, 66, 69, 89, 93, 176, 206,
      215
   Garlic and Herbs, Boursin, 155
   Gruyere, 55
   Mexican blend, 14, 18, 156
   Monterey jack, 245
   Parmesan, 17, 65, 103, 106, 135,
      149, 165
   queso fresco, 245
   Swiss, 76
Cherry pie filling, 201
Chicken, 100, 106
   breasts, 75, 118, 132
   cooked, 60, 103
   fryer, 117
   meatballs, cooked, 79

tenders, 109

wing drumettes, 83

Chocolate

chips, semisweet, 166, 172, 202, 205, 212, 220

Cocoa powder, unsweetened, 198

Coconut

flakes, 166

milk, 205

oil, 186

Cod, 96

Coleslaw mix, 46

Condensed milk, 215, 219

Cookies, chocolate sandwich, 166, 206, 216

Corn, 41

creamed, 42

frozen, 41, 190

Cornmeal, 109

Crackers, 83

Cranberries, dried, 127

D

Dates, 66

Dressing, Thousand island, 76

E

Eggplant, 152

Eggs, hard-boiled, 52, 59, 179

Evaporated milk, 156

G

Garlic, 55, 65, 118, 124, 139, 146, 152, 185, 234, 242

Gelatin, 194

Graham cracker(s), 220

crumbs, 212

crust, 215

Grouper, 160

H

Half-and-half, 42, 194

Ham, 31

Heavy cream, 24, 103, 149, 197, 198, 206, 211, 212, 216, 219

Herbs

basil, 56

chives, 229

cilantro, 23, 80, 190, 226, 230, 238, 241, 246

dill, 93

mint, 123, 124, 219

parsley, 128, 139, 185

rosemary, 106, 123

Honey, 83, 169, 186, 219, 226, 233, 234

I

Ice cream, 212, 216

J

Juice

lemon, 70, 93, 118, 124, 139

lime, 80, 86, 215, 226, 238, 241, 246

K

Kale, 135

Kosher salt (sea salt), 13, 14, 17, 18, 23, 24, 28, 31, 35, 36, 41, 42, 45, 46, 52, 55, 56, 59, 60, 70, 80, 86, 89, 90, 93, 96, 99, 100, 103, 106, 109, 110, 113, 117, 118, 123, 124, 127, 128, 131, 132, 135, 136, 139, 142, 145, 146, 152, 155, 156, 159, 160, 165, 169, 175, 176, 179, 180, 185, 186, 189, 190, 194, 219, 225, 226, 229, 230, 233, 234, 241, 242, 245, 246

L

Lamb

chops, 123

racks of, 124

Lemon(s), 100, 160

curd, 211

juice, see Juice

zest, 124

Lettuce, iceberg, 49

Limes, 230, 237

juice, see Juice

M

Mangos, 238

Maple syrup, 27, 128, 175

Marshmallows, 220

Mayonnaise, 45, 52, 65, 76, 96, 128, 176, 179, 229

Meringues, vanilla, 211
Mix
    pancake, 27
    yellow cake, 201
Mushrooms, 17
Mustard
    Dijon, 128, 145, 179
    yellow, 52

N
Nuts, roasted and salted, 172, 175

O
Oats, 186
Onions
    green, 36, 42, 45, 59, 79, 127, 179,
        180, 189, 237
    red, 41, 52, 86, 238
    sweet, 55
    yellow, 24, 31, 56, 65, 90, 113,
        131, 142, 245
    white, 90, 113, 131, 142, 241, 245,
        246

P
Pasta
    bow ties, 156
    elbows, 156
    fettuccine, 103
    fusilli, 106
    linguine, 135
    penne, 46, 106

spaghetti, 149, 152
    spirals, 156
Pears, 127, 131
Peas, baby frozen, 123
Pecans, 89, 201
Peppers, 142
    Anaheim chilies, 234
    ancho chili, 242
    chipotle, in adobo, 80
    jalapeño, 69, 89, 234, 241, 246
    pimentos, 176
    red bell, 31, 152
Pineapple, 45, 201
Pine nuts, 155
Pistachios, 124, 194
Popcorn kernels, 165
Pork
    baby back ribs, 114
    chops, 110, 127
    roast, 131, 146
    sausages, *see Sausages*
Potato(es)
    baby gold, 159
    chips, 96
    fingerling, 136
    French fries, frozen, 185
    hash browns, frozen, 14
    red, 146
    russet, 36, 180
    tater tots, frozen, 189
    tricolored small, 52
    Yukon Gold, 31, 42, 118, 123
    white, 113

Pretzel(s)
    miniature, 172
    sticks, 166

R
Raspberries, 197
Red snapper, 160
Rice, 172
    basmati or white, 230

S
Salsa, 18, 35, 159
    verde, 60
Salmon
    fillets, 128
    smoked, 93
Sauce
    barbecue, 75, 83, 90, 109, 113,
        114, 132, 142, 179
    chimichurri, 160
    chipotle in adobo, 226, 238
    hot, 79, 86, 100, 117, 175, 176, 189
    soy, 169
    tartar, 96
    Worcestershire, 89, 169
Sauerkraut, 76
Sausages
    breakfast, 13, 14
    Italian, sweet or spicy, 135, 136
    pork, 99
    turkey, 136
Shrimp, 70, 139
Sour cream, 56, 93, 180, 237

Spices
    Cajun seasoning, 36, 109
    chili powder, 169, 175, 245
        ancho, 225
        chipotle, 169
    cinnamon, 198
    cloves, ground, 242
    cumin, 35, 41, 60, 80, 226, 245
    garlic powder, 100, 110, 225, 229
    Italian seasoning, 99, 146
    onion powder, 225, 229
    paprika, 110, 117, 156
        smoked, 225
    poultry seasoning, 127
    red pepper flakes, 56, 118
    thyme, 136, 145

Spinach, 59, 155
Stock (broth)
    beef, 55, 145, 146, 159
    chicken, 35, 36, 60, 146
    vegetable, 35, 36

T

Tomatillos, 246
Tomato(es)
    and chilies, canned, 41, 113, 156, 190
    cherry, 46, 49, 99
    diced, canned 56
    fire roasted, canned, 152
    grape, 99
    Roma, 86, 241
    sun-dried, 155
Tortillas, corn, 18, 23

V

Vanilla extract, 194, 198, 202, 205, 206
Vinegar
    apple cider, 234
    balsamic, 55, 99, 135, 169
    red wine, 41, 52, 59, 99, 190
    white, 13, 234

Y

Yogurt, 233

Media Lab Books
For inquiries, call 646-838-6637

Copyright 2020 Topix Media Lab

Published by Topix Media Lab
14 Wall Street, Suite 4B
New York, NY 10005

Printed in Korea

ISBN-13: 978-1-948174-47-3
ISBN-10: 1-948174-47-2

CEO Tony Romando

Vice President & Publisher Phil Sexton
Senior Vice President of Sales & New Markets Tom Mifsud
Vice President of Retail Sales & Logistics Linda Greenblatt
Director of Finance Vandana Patel
Manufacturing Director Nancy Puskuldjian
Financial Analyst Matthew Quinn
Brand Marketing & Promotions Assistant Emily McBride

Chief Content Officer Jeff Ashworth
Director of Editorial Operations Courtney Kerrigan
Creative Director Steven Charny
Photo Director Dave Weiss
Executive Editor Tim Baker

Content Editor Juliana Sharaf
Art Director Susan Dazzo
Senior Editor Trevor Courneen
Designer Kelsey Payne
Copy Editor & Fact Checker Tara Sherman

Co-Founders Bob Lee, Tony Romando

JOHN WAYNE ENTERPRISES